THE PUSH
FOR SOCIAL
CHANGE

The Environmental Movement

Stuart A. Kallen

ReferencePoint
Press®

San Diego, CA

About the Author

Stuart A. Kallen is the author of more than 350 nonfiction books for children and young adults. He has written on topics ranging from the theory of relativity to the art of electronic dance music. In addition, Kallen has written award-winning children's videos and television scripts. In his spare time he is a singer, songwriter, and guitarist in San Diego.

© 2019 ReferencePoint Press, Inc.
Printed in the United States

For more information, contact:
ReferencePoint Press, Inc.
PO Box 27779
San Diego, CA 92198
www.ReferencePointPress.com

Picture Credits:
Cover: MundusImages/iStockphoto.com

4: Umberto Shtanzman/Shutterstock.com (top)
4: sumikophoto/Shutterstock.com (bottom left)
4: Emma Geary/Shutterstock.com (bottom right)
5: MaskaRad/Shutterstock.com (top)
5: Drop of Light/Shutterstock.com (middle)
5: photoguy22/iStockphoto.com (bottom)
8: Kenneth Song/ZUMA Press/Newscom
11: Associated Press
16: Mark Newman/Minden Pictures
19: Maks Ershov/Shutterstock.com
23: Associated Press
25: Associated Press

32: Everett Collection/Newscom
37: US President Ronald Reagan at a Press Conference, c.1985 (photo)/© Mirrorpix/ Bridgeman Images
39: Ryan McGurl/Shutterstock.com
43: step2626/iStock.com
50: Associated Press
53: Associated Press
57: imagesandstories/picture alliance/ blickwinkel/i/Newscom
62: Tom Stromme/The Bismarck Tribune/ Associated Press
64: Jeff Malet Photography/Newscom
69: Gene Blevins/Reuters/Newscom

LIBRARY OF CONGRESS CATALOGING-IN-PUBLICATION DATA

Name: Kallen, Stuart A., 1955– author.
Title: The Environmental Movement/by Stuart A. Kallen.
Description: San Diego, CA: ReferencePoint Press, Inc., 2019. | Series: The Push for Social Change | Includes bibliographical references and index.
Identifiers: LCCN 2017058278 (print) | LCCN 2018003992 (ebook) | ISBN 9781682824245 (eBook) | ISBN 9781682824238 (hardback)
Subjects: LCSH: Environmentalism—United States—History—Juvenile literature. | Environmental policy—United States—History—Juvenile literature. | Environmental protection—United States—History—Juvenile literature.
Classification: LCC GE195.5 (ebook) | LCC GE195.5 .K35 2019 (print) | DDC 363.700973—dc23
LC record available at https://lccn.loc.gov/2017058278

CONTENTS

IMPORTANT EVENTS OF THE ENVIRONMENTAL MOVEMENT

1969
An offshore oil well near Santa Barbara, California, leaks 3 million gallons (11.4 million L) of crude oil into the Pacific Ocean, killing sea life and soiling beaches.

1962
Rachel Carson's best-selling book *Silent Spring* educates the public about the dangers of DDT and other industrial chemicals.

1967
A group of conservationists from Long Island, New York, establishes the Environmental Defense Fund to protect the environment by means of lawsuits and legal actions.

1970
The first Earth Day is celebrated by 20 million people on April 22.

1960	1963	1966	1969	1972

1963
The Sierra Club battles the Bureau of Reclamation to halt construction of two dams that would submerge portions of the Grand Canyon.

1966
Air pollution in New York City on Thanksgiving weekend kills an estimated 168 people.

1971
President Richard Nixon signs the Clean Air Act to drastically reduce air pollution by establishing national standards for air quality.

1972
The Clean Water Act is passed to limit the flow of sewage and industrial chemicals into rivers, lakes, and streams.

1973
Congress passes the Endangered Species Act to safeguard threatened plants and animals.

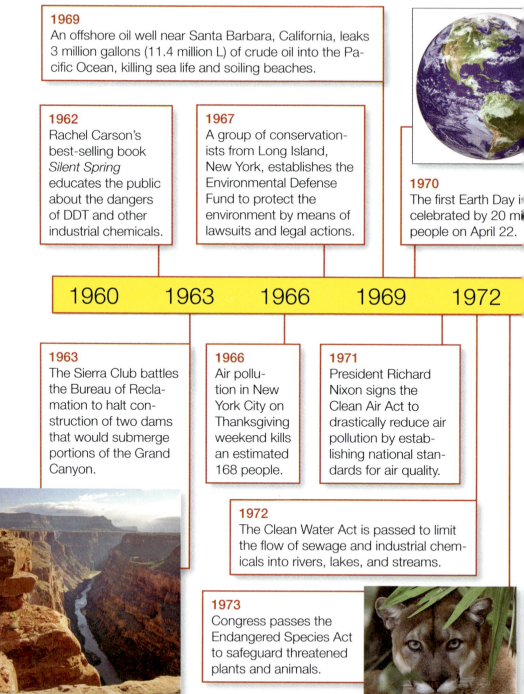

2014
The Intergovernmental Panel on Climate Change releases an alarming report that predicts serious environmental consequences if the world's nations do not immediately reduce greenhouse gas emissions.

1974
The Safe Drinking Water Act is passed to protect public health by ensuring the safety of drinking water.

2013
President Barack Obama issues an executive order to establish the President's Climate Action Plan, aimed at slowing the impact of climate change.

1992
The twelve-day Earth Summit is held in Rio de Janeiro, Brazil, to address the problem of climate change.

1975	1985	1995	2005	2015

1980
The radical environmental advocacy group Earth First! is founded in the Southwest.

2006
Former vice president Al Gore's documentary film *An Inconvenient Truth* helps raise public awareness about climate change.

2016
The Paris Agreement, aimed at reducing global greenhouse gas emissions, is signed by 195 countries.

1988
The antienvironmental Wise Use movement is established in Reno, Nevada.

2017
President Donald Trump pulls the United States out of the Paris Agreement while instituting plans for major increases in fossil fuel production.

1990
The twentieth anniversary of Earth Day is celebrated by 200 million people in 141 countries.

A Broad-Based Movement

On June 22, 1969, the Cuyahoga River in Cleveland, Ohio, burst into flames. Like many other major rivers in the Midwest at the time, the Cuyahoga was a toxic mess lined with oil refineries, paint factories, chemical plants, and steel foundries. These industrial producers poured 155 tons (141 metric tons) of hazardous waste into the river every day. A cover story in *Time* magazine described the state of the water: "Some River! Chocolate-brown, oily, bubbling with subsurface gases, it oozes rather than flows. 'Anyone who falls into the Cuyahoga does not drown,' Cleveland citizens joke grimly, 'he decays.' . . . The lower Cuyahoga has no visible signs of life, not even low forms such as leeches and sludge worms that usually thrive on wastes. It is also—literally—a fire hazard."[1] This was the tenth time since 1868 that the flammable waste in the Cuyahoga had caught fire. But it was the first to make national headlines.

Although it lasted only twenty minutes, the fire on the Cuyahoga River shined an unwelcome light on the environmental costs of the nation's industrial output. For decades Americans had been clear-cutting forests, mining for coal, drilling for oil, and creating vast amounts of air and water pollution while producing cars, steel, and plastics. Skies over major cities were dark with thick, choking smog. Rivers, lakes, and oceans were used as industrial sewers—contaminated with deadly chemicals that remain in the environment for decades. The bald eagle, a symbol of the nation's strength, was nearly extinct due to the adverse effects of the powerful pesticide DDT.

Sharing Common Values

The Cuyahoga River fire occurred during a time when millions of Americans regularly took to the streets to protest racism and the Vietnam War. The burning river incident inspired environmental activists of the era to use the tactics of the antiwar movement to focus the public's attention on the polluted environment. On April 22, 1970, rallies were held in streets, parks, and auditoriums to celebrate the first Earth Day. An estimated 20 million people—around one in ten Americans—attended Earth Day events. The coast-to-coast demonstration for a clean environment had a unifying effect. As the Earth Day Network website states: "Groups that had been fighting against oil spills, polluting factories and power plants, raw sewage, toxic dumps, pesticides, freeways, the loss of wilderness, and the extinction of wildlife suddenly realized they shared common values."[2]

After Earth Day numerous new environmental organizations were founded, including Friends of the Earth, the Natural Resources Defense Council, and Greenpeace. A new generation of magazines such as the *Whole Earth Catalog* and *Mother Earth News* taught Americans about recycling, organic gardening, renewable energy, and preserving the environment. In the years that followed, a loose confederation of individuals and groups from schoolkids to die-hard activists and multimillion-dollar green organizations formed an enduring broadbased movement dedicated to environmentalism. And the movement was not overtly political. In the early years the task of cleaning up the environment was bipartisan, supported by Democrats and Republicans alike.

Today people take clean air and water for granted, but new threats to the environment continued to emerge long after the floating oil slicks were cleaned up on the Cuyahoga River. Headlines in the 1980s described numerous environmental disasters in the

> "Groups that had been fighting against oil spills, polluting factories . . . and the extinction of wildlife suddenly realized they shared common values."[2]
>
> —Earth Day Network

making, including the widespread destruction of the Amazon rain forest in South America and global climate change caused by burning fossil fuels. Environmentalists educated the public about these problems in articles, interviews, documentaries, and testimony before Congress, creating a worldwide interest in environmentalism.

Environmentalists continue to address numerous threats as the fiftieth anniversary of Earth Day approaches. Record-setting droughts, wildfires, superstorms, and hurricanes are increasing in frequency as the climate continues to change. Millions of tons of plastic garbage contaminate the oceans, rain forests continue to fall, and air and water pollution in developing nations rivals anything seen in the United States in the 1960s. And advocates for environmental justice continue to fight pollution in communities of color.

A woman is rescued from her home after severe rainstorms triggered mudslides in California in 2018. Record-setting storms, droughts, and wildfires remind people that human activity can harm the environment.

Environmental Backlash

In the twenty-first century the environmental movement has become increasingly politicized. Some industry groups and politicians believe that laws protecting the environment go too far and are bad for job creation and the economy. In 2016 an antienvironmentalist named Scott Pruitt was chosen by President Donald Trump to run the US Environmental Protection Agency (EPA). Pruitt spent his career as attorney general of Oklahoma suing the EPA to block measures meant to reduce smog and curb climate-warming emissions from power plants. As Pruitt told the press when his nomination was announced, "The American people are tired of seeing billions of dollars drained from our economy due to unnecessary EPA regulations, and I intend to run this agency in a way that fosters . . . freedom for American businesses."[3]

> "I intend to run [the EPA] in a way that fosters . . . freedom for American businesses."[3]
>
> —Scott Pruitt, head of the EPA

Pruitt's view on environmental regulation is out of step with that of most Americans. A 2017 poll by the Pew Research Center showed that 74 percent of US adults agreed with the statement "the country should do whatever it takes to protect the environment." This compares with 23 percent who said "the country has gone too far in its efforts to protect the environment."[4] In addition, a 2017 Quinnipiac University poll showed 60 percent of Americans said the United States needs to do more to address climate change, compared with 35 percent who said the country is doing enough or too much. Surveys show that more than half of all Americans believe protecting the environment should be the top priority for the Trump administration and Congress.

Whatever the views of politicians, the majority of Americans—and people in countries all over the world—support environmental protection whatever the cost. These widely held beliefs are the legacy of an environmental movement that has been educating the public and fighting for a cleaner planet for more than half a century.

CHAPTER ONE

Creating a Movement

Rachel Carson was a marine biologist who wrote two best-selling books in the 1950s about ocean life. Carson's third book, *Silent Spring*, published in 1962, engrossed the reading public from the opening chapter, titled "A Fable for Tomorrow." Carson described a pastoral town in America's heartland where puffy white clouds drifted over prosperous farms surrounded by wheat fields, orchards, wildflowers, shrubs, and oak, maple, and pine trees. Foxes barked in the hills, deer wandered silently across fields, birds sang in the trees, and streams rippled with trout. All life existed in harmony. But as the tale continued, the picture darkened:

> A strange blight crept over the area and everything began to change. Some evil spell had settled on the community: mysterious maladies swept the flocks of chickens; the cattle and sheep sickened and died. Everywhere was a shadow of death. The farmers spoke of much illness among their families. . . . [Children] would be stricken suddenly while at play and die within a few hours. There was a strange stillness. The birds, for example—where had they gone?[5]

Carson then revealed what released the shadow of death on the earth—a granular white powder called DDT. The pesticide was responsible for the spring without birdsong—the silent spring.

While no community had suffered all of the troubles of Carson's fabled town, numerous communities had experienced problems like those she described. Highly toxic DDT was sprayed indiscriminately throughout the world starting in the late 1940s. During an era when there was a widespread fear of nuclear war, Carson pointed out that "no enemy action had silenced the rebirth of new life in this stricken world. The people had done it themselves."[6]

Selling an Insect Bomb

DDT is short for "dichlorodiphenyltrichloroethane." The chemical was first approved for commercial use by the US Department of Agriculture in 1945. Companies that produced DDT advertised it as a miraculous insect bomb. Farmers could greatly increase yields by spraying the inexpensive pesticide on all their crops. Chemical companies advertised that DDT was safe and non-toxic and would protect families from disease-carrying fleas, cockroaches, mosquitoes, flies, and lice. By the 1950s Americans were annually spraying more than 125 million pounds (57 million kg) of DDT around their homes and on fields, forests, waterways, and roadside vegetation.

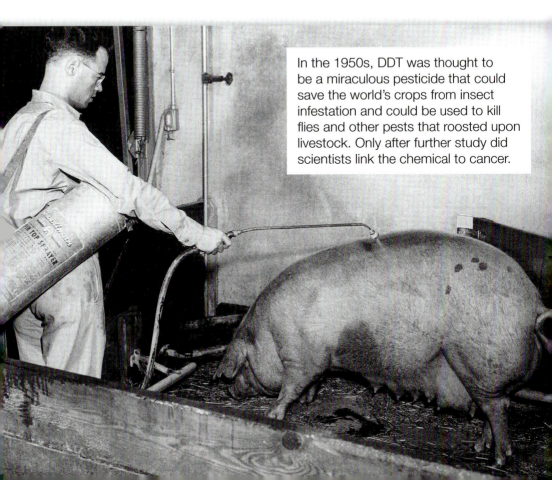

In the 1950s, DDT was thought to be a miraculous pesticide that could save the world's crops from insect infestation and could be used to kill flies and other pests that roosted upon livestock. Only after further study did scientists link the chemical to cancer.

Despite the advertised promises, the effects of DDT on human health and the environment had barely been studied. And DDT killed beneficial insects as well as those considered pests. Widespread use of the chemical could harm animals that depended on insects for food. As nature writer Edwin Way Teale warned in 1945: "Ninety percent of all insects are good, and if they are killed, things go out of kilter right away."[7]

DDT in the Environment

By the time Carson began writing *Silent Spring* in the late 1950s, researchers were starting to understand the problems associated with DDT. The chemical was thought to cause cancer in humans and was linked to serious reproductive problems among populations of birds, fish, bees, frogs, pigs, chickens, and cows. Carson used this research to make a case against DDT in language that the average reader could easily understand. She explained how industry was inventing and marketing hundreds of new synthetic chemicals every year that were as toxic as DDT. Many of these chemicals were used by farmers to kill insects, weeds, rodents, fungus, and other organisms. Carson noted that the chemicals were carried on the winds and rain and lingered in the soil for decades:

> [The chemicals] have been found in fish in remote mountain lakes, in earthworms burrowing in soil, in the eggs of birds — and in man himself. For these chemicals are now stored in the bodies of the vast majority of human beings, regardless of age. They occur in the mother's milk, and probably in the tissues of the unborn child. . . . If we are going to live so intimately with these chemicals — eating and drinking them, taking them into the very marrow of our bones — we had better know something about their nature and their power.[8]

Carson described how DDT works its way through the food chain. After being dusted on crops fed to livestock, molecules of DDT are stored in the fat, muscle, and organs of farm animals. When people consume those animals, the concentrated chemicals enter the body, where they are stored throughout a person's life. Carson noted, "This situation . . . means that today the average individual almost certainly starts life with the first deposit of the growing load of [DDT] his body will be required to carry thenceforth."[9]

Rachel Carson's Case Against Insecticides

Marine biologist and best-selling author Rachel Carson was well regarded for her ability to explain scientific concepts in easily understood terms. In the following excerpt from *Silent Spring*, Carson describes the problem with DDT and other agricultural chemicals.

> Since the mid-1940s over 200 basic chemicals have been created for use in killing insects, weeds, rodents, and other organisms described in the modern vernacular as "pests"; and they are sold under several thousand different brand names. These sprays, dusts, and aerosols are now applied almost universally to farms, gardens, forests, and homes—nonselective chemicals that have the power to kill every insect, the "good" and the "bad," to still the song of birds and the leaping of fish in the streams, to coat the leaves with a deadly film, and to linger on in soil—all this though the intended target may be only a few weeds or insects. Can anyone believe it is possible to lay down such a barrage of poisons on the surface of the earth without making it unfit for all life? They should not be called "insecticides," but "biocides." The whole process of spraying seems caught up in an endless spiral. . . . Insects, in a triumphant vindication of Darwin's principle of the survival of the fittest, have evolved super races immune to the particular insecticide used, hence a deadlier one has always to be developed—and then a deadlier one than that. . . . Thus the chemical war is never won, and all life is caught in its violent crossfire.

Rachel Carson, *Silent Spring*. Greenwich, CT: Crest, 1962, pp. 12–13.

Challenging the Chemical Industry

Silent Spring went on to sell 2 million copies. Carson's words alarmed the public; thousands of readers contacted their congressional representatives to demand an immediate halt to DDT production. This brought a swift negative reaction from DDT promoters, including scientists, bureaucrats, and representatives of the chemical and food industries. There were fears that if DDT were banned, the public would lose confidence in all of the chemical industry's products and expensive new testing procedures might be put in place. And the criticism of DDT also had cultural repercussions, as Carson biographer Linda Lear explains: "[*Silent Spring* was] a fundamental social critique of a gospel of technological progress. Carson had attacked the integrity of the scientific establishment, its moral leadership, and its direction of society. . . . She dared to make their sins public."[10]

On television and in newspapers, magazines, and brochures, the chemical industry and its allies orchestrated an attack on Carson. Her integrity and even her sanity were publicly questioned. The chemical company Monsanto handed out thousands of brochures claiming that a worldwide famine would ensue if DDT was banned.

Carson had anticipated the industry reaction; she included fifty-five pages of footnotes in *Silent Spring* that backed her findings. The book also contained a list of experts who approved of the book's conclusions. And the chemical industry attacks on Carson helped increase public awareness of the dangers of pesticides. When the television news program *CBS Reports* broadcast the special *The Silent Spring of Rachel Carson* in 1963, an estimated 15 million viewers tuned in. Carson calmly discussed the implications of her work in measured tones: "Man's attitude toward nature is today critically important simply because we have now acquired a fateful power to alter and destroy nature. But man is a part of nature, and his war against nature is inevitably a war against himself."[11] After the show aired, President John F. Kennedy ordered the President's Science Advisory Committee to study DDT and other pesticides. Carson testified before the committee, which issued a report in 1963 backing her scientific claims.

> "Man is a part of nature, and his war against nature is inevitably a war against himself."[11]
>
> —Rachel Carson, marine biologist and author

Silent Spring is considered a seminal book that galvanized conservationists, biologists, scientists, social critics, and average citizens to join the environmental movement. The book was translated into dozens of languages, which helped lay the foundation for the worldwide green movement. As environmental engineer and Carson scholar H. Patricia Hynes explains, "*Silent Spring* altered the balance of power in the world. No one since would be able to sell pollution as the necessary underside of progress so easily or uncritically."[12] Carson, however, would not live to see the revolution she started. At the time *Silent Spring* was published, she had been suffering from breast cancer for several years. Carson died on April 14, 1964, at age fifty-six.

Defending Birds with Science and Law

As *Silent Spring* made clear, DDT was killing birds. Scientists who studied birds—called ornithologists—were compiling research that proved large bird populations were rapidly declining. Raptors like bald eagles, peregrine falcons, hawks, ospreys, and others were nearing extinction. Their eggs had shells that were so thin they broke when the mothers sat on them. This was due to the prevalence of DDT in the environment. Researchers also found DDT spraying caused songbirds like finches, sparrows, and robins to have seizures and die.

In 1965 a loose affiliation of around thirty scientists, lawyers, ornithologists, and college students based in Long Island, New York, decided to launch a legal battle against DDT. The group,

Because DDT stayed in living cells, the toxin traveled up the food chain, passing from prey to predator. Bald eagles, for example, suffered declining populations from the poison, which weakened the eggshells of unhatched young and resulted in the deaths of many embryos.

which would take the name Environmental Defense Fund (EDF) in 1967 was inspired by Carson's words. They laid out a unique strategy that had never been attempted and was considered radical at the time. The activists would link legal concepts about property rights with detailed scientific research about DDT. The goal was to take on one of the most powerful industries in the world. As one member of the group, biologist Charles Wurster, later explained, "We [thought] that marrying science and law to defend the environment in court was a good strategy. Courts had not been used for environmental protection before."[13]

The activists filed a lawsuit in the New York State Supreme Court against a Long Island government bureau: the Suffolk County Mosquito Commission, which had been spraying DDT in local marshes and coastal wetlands for nearly twenty years. For about ten of those years, Suffolk County citizens had been trying to halt spraying by writing letters to newspapers and their congressional representatives. These efforts had not worked. But a few weeks after the lawsuit was filed, a New York State Supreme Court judge ordered the Suffolk County Mosquito Commission to stop using DDT.

The efforts of the activists attracted widespread interest, and the public soon started sending unsolicited donations to the EDF. However, the case was not resolved. The powerful chemical industry appealed the ruling. A federal district court judge ruled that the EDF did not have "standing"—the right to sue the government—because the group did not have a financial stake in the outcome. In other words, the EDF would not benefit if DDT was banned. As Wurster later said, "We were fighting to protect birds. Birds had no standing in court, so we could not represent them since we were not birds. But we . . . realized that filing lawsuits could be a powerful tool."[14]

> "We [thought] that marrying science and law to defend the environment in court was a good strategy."[13]
>
> —Charles Wurster, biologist

In 1970, after losing its case in district court, the EDF appealed to the US Court of Appeals in Washington, DC, the second-highest court in the country. The court issued a ruling in the EDF's favor. Although the chemical industry continued to fight the case, the federal government banned the use of DDT in the United States in 1972. Wurster explains the importance of the EDF's battle: "It helped create a body of judicial decisions that would form the foundation of environmental law. It helped knock down the legal barriers that prevented citizens from suing the government. Other organizations started using litigation as well and it gave the environmental community an effective tool."[15]

The Fight Against Grand Canyon Dams

The legal case against DDT was aided by the fact that the American public largely supported the ban. Public opinion also helped drive another great victory for environmentalists in the 1960s. The

Sierra Club convinced Americans to oppose the construction of two dams on the Colorado River that would have flooded parts of Grand Canyon National Park. The battle against the dams was led by environmentalist, adventurer, and author Martin Litton. The conflict was notable because it pitted a then small environmental organization against a powerful federal agency, the Bureau of Reclamation, which oversaw construction of numerous dams, power plants, and canals in the western United States.

The fight began in 1963 when Litton learned of the bureau's plans to flood Marble Canyon. This remote 60-mile (97 km) section of the Colorado River was located at the eastern boundary of Grand Canyon National Park. Marble Canyon was known for its exquisite beauty. When explorer John Wesley Powell first mapped the canyon in 1869, he wrote, "The limestone of this canyon is often polished, and . . . sometimes the rocks are of many colors—whites, gray, pink, and purple, with saffron tints."[16] Despite the canyon's reputation as one of the most magnificent gorges on earth, the Bureau of Reclamation viewed it as an excellent place to build a dam that would provide cheap hydroelectric power to the Southwest and store freshwater for use by Phoenix and Tucson, Arizona.

The bureau also had plans for a second dam on the Colorado River that would have flooded Bridge Canyon on the western edge of the Grand Canyon. Together the Bridge Canyon and Marble Canyon dams would create two standing lakes that would submerge 130 miles (209 km) of the Colorado River gorge with water up to 500 hundred feet (152 m) deep in some places. While most Americans had never heard of Bridge Canyon or Marble Canyon, Litton was very familiar with both. As a river runner he had often paddled down the rapids that ran through the canyons.

The Sierra Club was a small organization when it took on the Bureau of Reclamation; it had only around twenty-two thousand members, mostly on the West Coast. Each of these members received a monthly newsletter, the *Sierra Club Bulletin*. In 1963 Litton used the bulletin to make a case against the dams. He noted that dividing the Colorado River into three segments, as

In the early 1960s, the Sierra Club organized an effective grassroots resistance to the damming of the Colorado River and the subsequent flooding of Arizona's Marble Canyon. Though a small group at the time, the Sierra Club successfully persuaded lawmakers to end the project in 1966.

the dams would do, would invariably injure the ecosystem of the Grand Canyon. Litton appealed to Sierra Club members to deluge federal representatives with protest letters:

> Shall we fail to go into battle because it is hard to win? Could not 22,000 Sierra Club members, without strain, turn out 22,000 letters a day for a week? . . . There has never been a Congress, a President, a Secretary of Interior, a governor or a newspaper editor who would not sit up and take notice of that kind of mail. . . . [Seven] letters each . . . and more to follow could assure the Canyon's interim survival and rescue the opportunity for reason to prevail.[17]

Rallying the Public

At the end of the essay, Litton included the names and addresses of all the officeholders mentioned, including the president. It is

Environmental Warrior Martin Litton

Martin Litton was born near Los Angeles in Gardena, California, in 1917. At that time the public largely supported damming the wild rivers of the West to provide irrigation and cheap hydroelectricity. Litton, who spent a great deal of time exploring western rivers in small wooden boats called dories, did not agree. In 1952 he helped launch the environmental movement as it is known today. He worked with the Sierra Club to mobilize public opinion against the construction of two dams that would have submerged 110 miles (177 km) of scenic canyons in Dinosaur National Monument in northeastern Utah. The project was dropped in 1954. A decade later, Litton was behind the grassroots campaign that prevented the Bureau of Reclamation from building two dams on the Colorado River that would have flooded parts of Grand Canyon National Park.

In later years Litton campaigned for the creation of Redwood National Park in Northern California and fought a Disney resort planned near Sequoia National Park in the central part of the state. At age eighty-seven he set a record as the oldest man ever to row a dory through the Grand Canyon. He was a tough and combative force who took on the government and won. When Litton died in 2014 at age ninety-seven, Barbara Boyle of the Sierra Club summed up the pioneer of the environmental movement as "passionate, original, tempestuous, stubborn, charming, obnoxious, courteous, inappropriate, dogged, fiery, and impossibly effective."

Quoted in National Geographic, "Appreciation: Lessons from the Man Who Stopped the Grand Canyon Dams," December 12, 2014. https://news.nationalgeographic.com.

unknown how many people actually wrote to their representatives, but the Sierra Club campaign against the dams continued. The group published a large book, *Time and the River Flowing: Grand Canyon*, that featured spectacular color photographs of the gorge, a narrative about rafting through the canyon, and arguments against the dam.

In 1965 press coverage of the issue increased after Sierra Club president David Brower convinced national publications such as the *New York Times*, *Time*, and *Life* to write articles about the destructive effects of the proposed dams. Although the articles generated publicity for the cause, the Sierra Club was fighting powerful politicians and bureaucrats determined to build the dams. In 1966 Brower made what was then considered a controversial move: The Sierra Club took out full-page ads in the *New York Times* and *Wash-*

ington Post with the headline "Now Only You Can Save the Grand Canyon from Being Flooded . . . for Profit." The ad contained ten points about the dams and the canyons, the names of politicians supporting the dams, and arguments against the project. The ad concluded, "Remember . . . there is only one simple, incredible issue here: This time it's the Grand Canyon they want to flood. *The Grand Canyon*."[18] The ad contained addresses of representatives, the secretary of the interior, the president, and others. The public responded. The letters poured in, phones rang in congressional offices, and newspapers covered the story. The following week the bill to authorize construction of the dams was defeated in Congress.

The anti-dam campaign swelled Sierra Club membership. By 1968 membership had increased to more than seventy-eight thousand people. In 1969 President Lyndon B. Johnson established the Marble Canyon National Monument, which protected the area. In 1975 Marble Canyon was added to Grand Canyon National Park. Bridge Canyon is now part of the Hualapai Indian Reservation.

> "When it comes to saving wilderness, we can't be extreme enough. To compromise is to lose."[19]
>
> —Martin Litton, environmentalist

No Reason to Be Reasonable

There were a number of similarities between the Grand Canyon battle and the fight against DDT. Both issues pitted powerful moneyed interests against committed activists who attracted public support through the media. And the issues that were brought to light laid the groundwork for the movement to protect the environment that would spread throughout the world in the decade that followed. In 2010 Litton continued to defend the tactics used in the Grand Canyon campaign: "People always tell me not to be extreme. 'Be reasonable!' they say. But I never felt it did any good to be reasonable about anything in conservation, because what you give away will never come back—ever. When it comes to saving wilderness, we can't be extreme enough. To compromise is to lose."[19]

CHAPTER TWO

Working for Cleaner Air and Water

During the 1960s millions of American lived in cities where the air was a brown haze of pollution that burned the eyes, irritated the lungs, and heightened the risk of heart disease, stroke, cancer, and other diseases. New York City, Pittsburgh, Chicago, Houston, and Los Angeles were choked by a sickening mix of carbon monoxide, nitrogen dioxide, and hydrocarbons emitted by cars and trucks. Coal-burning power plants and steel mills disgorged millions of tons of sulfur dioxide, creating forest-killing acid rain that was nearly as corrosive as vinegar. Plastic factories discharged a miasma of air pollutants, and in many municipal landfills, garbage was simply burned in the open air. While some basic state and federal laws regulated air pollution, they were mostly ignored.

Air pollution was so bad that periodic temperature inversions created public emergencies. Inversions happen when warm air—and pollution—is trapped on the ground by a layer of cold air pushing down from above. For three days over Thanksgiving weekend in 1966, millions of people in New York City suffered from a temperature inversion. An estimated 168 people died from heart attacks and respiratory failure. Researchers later determined that an additional 360 New Yorkers suffered cardiac and respiratory problems from the smog event that significantly shortened their lives. Air pollution researcher William Wise described what he saw flying over New York City during the inversion: "We were flying at about two thousand feet, through a curiously greasy-looking and pervasive haze. . . . Cars, roads, houses, the very earth itself had been blotted out. . . . The smog extended to the horizon in every direction . . . yellow and ugly, like nothing so much as a vast and unappetizing sea of chicken soup."[20] What Wise described was the third record-setting air pollution disaster to hit New York City; similar events occurred in 1953 and 1963.

Even when records were not being set, bad air quality was simply a fact of life during much of the twentieth century. And dirty air was just part of the pollution story. Steel and paper mills, chemical plants, paint factories, meatpacking plants, landfills, and wastewater treatment facilities used rivers and lakes as industrial sewers. The Great Lakes, which hold 20 percent of all freshwater on earth, were so polluted that Lake Erie was described as dead by *Time* magazine in 1969. The Hudson River, which flows past New York City, was so contaminated by human waste that the water contained bacteria levels 170 times above a limit considered safe for swimming and fishing.

> **"The smog extended to the horizon in every direction . . . yellow and ugly, like nothing so much as a vast and unappetizing sea of chicken soup."[20]**
>
> —William Wise, pollution researcher

Los Angeles was a chief target for activists seeking to bring attention to the problem of smog in America's cities during the 1960s. Blaming auto exhaust pipes and industrial smokestacks for such visible pollution, environmental groups helped convince the public to call for cleaner air.

Like dirty air, people had long viewed water pollution as the cost of living in a modern society. But by the end of the 1960s, the public was growing increasingly angry about the unregulated pollution spewing into the air and water. A chorus of voices rose up to demand that the government do something to preserve and protect the earth for future generations. A 1970 Gallup poll demonstrates the rising public support for environmentalism. In 1965 only 17 percent of Americans cited cleaning up the water and air as their top national priority. By 1970 that number was 53 percent. This led to what is commonly referred to as the environmental decade. This was a time when the environmental movement led numerous successful campaigns to create a significantly cleaner world. Many of the landmark federal laws passed during the decade, including the Clean Air Act, the Clean Water Act, and others, have been strengthened over the years and remain in place today.

The Santa Barbara Oil Spill

While many isolated incidents created momentum for the environmental decade, one event in particular is credited with shifting public opinion. A massive oil spill off the coast of Santa Barbara, California, fouled pristine beaches and called into question America's love of large gas-guzzling automobiles. On the morning of January 29, 1969, reporter Bob Sollen of the *Santa Barbara News-Press* received an anonymous phone call from someone who said, "The ocean is boiling."[21] The caller was referring to a blowout at an offshore Union Oil petroleum drilling platform 6 miles (10 km) from Santa Barbara. The accident unleashed a torrent of oil and gas into the Pacific Ocean. Within days Santa Barbara beaches were transformed, as local surfer Bud Bottoms recalls: "After the blowout you'd go to the beach and you couldn't hear the waves. Because all the coast was black [with oil]. . . . There was no noise of

"All the coast was black [with oil]. . . . There was no noise of the waves breaking. Just slop, slop, slop, slop. And people just stood there and cried."[22]

—Bud Bottoms, Santa Barbara resident

Work crews attempt to clean up a Santa Barbara beach in 1969 after an oil spill from an offshore drilling platform polluted coastal waters and washed onto the shore. The disaster coated the feathers of sea birds and the fur of aquatic mammals, causing numerous wildlife deaths.

the waves breaking. Just slop, slop, slop, slop. And people just stood there and cried. All our beaches were black."[22] News of the oil spill quickly made national headlines. The disaster also attracted international attention as grim images of dying oil-soaked pelicans, seals, and other marine animals circulated throughout the world.

Oil continued to pour out of the damaged well for more than four months, resulting in an estimated 3 million gallons (11.4 million L) of crude oil polluting the Pacific Ocean. In what was then the largest oil spill in US history, over 800 square miles (2,072 sq. km) of ocean was fouled, while tarred beaches stretched for 35 miles (56 km) along the California coastline. Before it was over, an estimated thirty-six hundred seabirds were killed, along with countless dolphins, seals, otters, and other creatures. People were shocked and saddened by the accident, and their anger was heightened by a statement from Union Oil president Fred Hartley, who told a

The Declaration of Environmental Rights

In 1969 Roderick Frazier Nash, a thirty-year-old assistant college professor at University of California–Santa Barbara (UCSB), wrote the Declaration of Environmental Rights. This primary document of the modern environmental movement is excerpted below.

> All men have the right to an environment capable of sustaining life and promoting happiness. If the accumulated actions of the past become destructive of this right men now living have the further right to repudiate the past for the benefit of the future. . . .
>
> Moved by an environmental disaster in the Santa Barbara Channel to think and act in national and world terms, we submit these charges:
>
> We have littered the land with refuse. . . .
>
> We have stripped the forest and the grasses and reduced the soil to fruitless dust.
>
> We have contaminated the air we breathe for life.
>
> We have befouled the lakes and rivers and oceans along with their shorelines. . . .
>
> Recognizing that the ultimate remedy for these fundamental problems is found in man's mind, not his machines, we call on societies and their governments to recognize and implement the following principles:
>
> We need an ecological consciousness that recognizes man as member, not master, of the community of living things sharing his environment. . . .
>
> We must find the courage to take upon ourselves as individuals responsibility for the welfare of the whole environment, treating our own back yards as if they were the world and the world as if it were our back yard. . . .
>
> Today is the first day of the rest our life on this planet. We will begin anew.

Roderick Frazier Nash, "Santa Barbara's Black Tide of 1969," American Institute for Progressive Democracy, 2015. http://taipd.org.

reporter, "I am always tremendously impressed at the publicity that death of birds receives versus the loss of people. . . . Although it has been referred to as a disaster, it is not a disaster to people."[23]

Hartley's callous comments served only to motivate Santa Barbara citizens to join a local grassroots environmental group called Get Oil Out!, or GOO. The group printed bumper stickers and pamphlets calling for a halt to all offshore oil drilling in California. GOO petitions received two hundred thousand signatures from people all over the United States. The group filled two hundred small bottles with oil and sent them to state and federal legislators. As the chorus of protest rose, the disaster attracted the attention of President Richard Nixon, who ordered a cessation of oil drilling in the waters off Santa Barbara on February 6, 1969. When the president toured a blackened Santa Barbara beach several weeks later, he remarked that the "incident has frankly touched the conscience of the American people."[24]

Declaration of Environmental Rights

Several Santa Barbara residents who helped clean up oil-soaked beaches and wildlife went on to become leaders in the environmental movement. Roderick Frazier Nash, a thirty-year-old assistant professor at the University of California–Santa Barbara (UCSB), watched the oil contaminate the local beaches in the days after the blowout. The experience moved him to compose a manifesto he called the Declaration of Environmental Rights. The document, which Nash based on the Declaration of Independence, proclaimed that people and animals had an absolute right to a clean and healthy environment. In January 1970, on the one-year anniversary of the Santa Barbara oil spill, Nash stood on a local beach and read the declaration to a national television audience. By this time Nash had created an interdisciplinary major at UCSB called environmental studies. Nash chaired the program for five years, and today that program is the oldest college curriculum of its kind in the United States.

Other influential Santa Barbara environmentalists and members of GOO included Denis Hayes, Selma Rubin, Marc McGinnes, and Bud Bottoms. Their prominent protests attracted the attention of Gaylord Nelson, a nature-loving Democratic senator from Wisconsin. Nelson scheduled a flight over the Santa Barbara oil spill and was horrified by the damage he viewed from the airplane window. While completing his flight to San Francisco, Nelson read a newspaper article about antiwar protesters who held "teach-ins" on college campuses. Those who organized teach-ins used them to educate students about the war the United States was waging in Vietnam. Nelson decided to hold a nationwide teach-in, a one-time event called Earth Day, to discuss environmentalism with students.

Nelson joined forces with Representative Pete McCloskey, a California Republican and an ardent environmentalist, to form a group called Environmental Teach-In. On September 20, 1969, Nelson held a national news conference to announce plans for a coast-to-coast teach-in the following spring. By the next day the Environmental Teach-In offices were inundated with phone calls from excited citizens who wanted to participate. With the movement gaining momentum, the teach-in idea was dropped. Instead, the group would encourage people to act locally to solve environmental problems on Earth Day, which would be held on April 22, 1970. Hayes, one of the coordinators, explained the concept:

> People could work on whatever was important to them: If your group was concerned about a freeway that was poised to cut through an inner-city neighborhood, then your Earth Day is just about fighting freeways. If you decided the internal combustion engine was the culprit for all that smog in Los Angeles and you wanted to pound an internal combustion engine apart with the sledgehammer, you could do that.[25]

Finding Common Ground

The first Earth Day event exceeded all the expectations of the organizers. In what was then the largest demonstration of any kind

Gaylord Nelson

Gaylord Nelson was a leading figure in the environmental movement whose efforts to protect air, water, land, and wildlife led to the creation of the annual Earth Day celebration. Nelson was born in 1916 in the northwestern Wisconsin town of Clear Lake. After earning a law degree, Nelson was elected to the Wisconsin State Senate in 1948. In 1958 Nelson was elected governor and became known as the "conservation governor." During his term, Nelson created the Outdoor Recreation Action Program, which acquired large tracts of land that were later converted to public parks and wilderness areas.

In 1962 Nelson was elected to the US Senate, where he sponsored environmental programs aimed at addressing social problems. For example, Operation Mainstream created conservation jobs for disadvantaged youth. However, Nelson quickly realized that few senators were interested in addressing environmental problems, and it would take the insistence of people, not politicians, to clean up the air and water. In 1970, inspired by the campus activism of the era, Nelson organized the first Earth Day to support grassroots environmental actions. Earth Day attracted 20 million Americans to demonstrations across the country. The event was a watershed moment that moved Congress to pass numerous environmental laws. In the 1960s and 1970s, Nelson helped write laws, including the Clean Water Act, the Clean Air Act, the National Wild and Scenic Rivers Act, the Federal Environmental Pesticide Control Act, and the National Trails System Act.

in US history, around one in ten Americans—20 million people—took part in Earth Day actions. Events were held in thousands of communities across the country. Classes were canceled at ten thousand public schools and on two thousand college campuses to celebrate the Earth. In big cities the streets were filled with tens of thousands of people who carried signs, listened to speeches, and signed petitions to support a cleaner environment. And the event was a bipartisan movement; Democrats, Republicans, and Independents alike celebrated Earth Day side by side. As Nelson explained after the event, "A new movement had begun, and uncounted millions—students, laborers, farmers, housewives, politicians, professional people, liberals and conservatives—who might have found it difficult to find common agreement on any other subject, were gathering together in a massive educational effort to talk about survival and the quality of survival in a world we all share."[26]

A New Agency to Repair the Damage

Perhaps nothing better demonstrated the growing political power of the environmental movement than the creation of the EPA on December 2, 1970. Like those of other environmental initiatives at the time, the roots of the EPA can be traced back to the Santa Barbara oil spill and Nelson. About a month after the oil spill, the US Congress had passed a bill called the National Environmental Policy Act (NEPA). The purpose of NEPA was stated in the bill's preamble: "To declare national policy which will encourage productive and enjoyable harmony between man and his environment; to promote efforts which will prevent or eliminate damage to the environment and biosphere and stimulate the health and welfare of man; to enrich the understanding of the ecological systems and natural resources important to the Nation."[27] NEPA established the Council on Environmental Quality (CEQ) to advise the president on environmental issues. The law also required all government agencies to create environmental impact statements whenever federal projects were planned, including the construction of highways, dams, and other infrastructure.

"A new movement had begun, and uncounted millions . . . were gathering together in a massive educational effort to talk about survival and the quality of survival in a world we all share."[26]

—Gaylord Nelson, Earth Day founder

The president, Richard Nixon, was a Republican who was known as a friend to big business. But Nixon's popularity was waning due to the growing public disapproval of the Vietnam War. As Santa Barbara environmentalist Paul Relis explains: "Nixon was prompted to adopt a more environmental position because he was so unpopular with the young."[28] Hoping to improve his standing, Nixon made a show of signing NEPA into law on January 1, 1970, as "my first official act in this new decade."[29]

Almost a year after signing NEPA, Nixon created the EPA with an executive order. Before the agency was founded, according to a global nonprofit leadership organization, "The national government was not structured to make a coordinated attack on the pollutants that harm human health and degrade the environment. The EPA was assigned the daunting task of repairing the damage already done to the natural environment and to establish new criteria to guide Americans in making a cleaner environment a reality."[30]

The EPA was tasked with conducting environmental research, instituting environmental protection standards, and combating pollution. The powerful government agency would enforce air and water pollution regulations, control the use of pesticides, oversee solid waste management, and establish clean drinking water standards. The first EPA administrator, thirty-eight-year-old assistant attorney general William D. Ruckelshaus, quickly became known in the press as Mr. Clean. On December 11, little more than a week after the EPA was founded, Ruckelshaus took on three cities with notable water pollution problems: Detroit, Atlanta, and Cleveland, the latter where hazardous waste catching fire on the Cuyahoga River in June 1969 had made headlines. The EPA head gave the cities six months to initiate plans to clean up their water.

Clean Air, Clean Water

On January 1, 1971, exactly one year after Nixon signed NEPA, the president signed the Clean Air Act, a major piece of environmental legislation that led to substantial changes in the air quality in cities across the country. The Clean Air Act established national standards for air quality and included tough enforcement provisions that took aim at polluters. Major corporations such as chemical manufacturer Union Carbide were ordered to reduce sulfur dioxide emissions by up to 70 percent within a year. Automakers were also forced to make major changes. The Clean Air

Act required all new cars sold after 1974 to emit 90 percent less pollution. For the first time, cars would be equipped with catalytic converters to convert exhaust gases into less toxic emissions.

The growing power of the environmental movement was behind a second major piece of legislation later passed by Congress. The Clean Water Act of 1972 dramatically changed the way rivers, lakes, and streams were regulated in the United States. The

The Clean Water Act is directly responsible for the reclamation of the once-polluted Cuyahoga River (pictured circa 1973) in Ohio. Today, the river is part of a government-protected ecosystem.

Clean Water Act required the EPA to identify and prevent point-source pollution. This is pollution discharged from a single identifiable source, such as an oil refinery, paint factory, or sewage treatment plant. The goal of the Clean Water Act was to reduce point-source pollution discharges to zero by setting limits on the acceptable amount of pollution that could be released into American waterways. Factories and municipal waste-treatment plants were required to use what the Clean Water Act called the "best available technology" to limit or eliminate pollution discharges in wastewater.

Two years later Congress passed the Safe Drinking Water Act of 1974 to protect public health. When the act went into effect, more than one-third of all tap water in the United States contained unsafe levels of hazardous chemicals. The Safe Drinking Water Act required 150,000 public water systems across the United States to drastically reduce levels of industrial toxins, chemicals, heavy metals, and bacteria in drinking water.

> "[Earth Day] created a seemingly unstoppable force that continued for the next four or five or six years—we had the Clean Air Act, the Clean Water Act, the Safe Drinking Water Act. . . . Just, bam, bam, bam, bam."[31]
>
> —Denis Hayes, environmental activist

A Lasting Impact

By the end of the 1970s, the Clean Water Act, the Clean Air Act, and other laws called for by the environmental movement were responsible for a profound improvement in the quality of life for average Americans. As Denis Hayes recalled: "[Earth Day] helped create the context in which the Clean Air Act passed overwhelmingly. It just created a seemingly unstoppable force that continued for the next four or five or six years—we had the Clean Air Act, the Clean Water Act, the Safe Drinking Water Act. . . . Just, bam, bam, bam, bam. We were striking while the iron was hot."[31]

The laws were effective because of an important EPA rule. The agency was required by law to make public notice of any proposed change in any environmental law. The agency had to hold open hearings and compile written comments from the public. Environmental history professor Cody Ferguson explains the importance of these requirements: "The inclusion of public notice and participation requirements in all of these laws, including the ability of citizens to appeal agency decisions, enhanced not only environmental regulations and protections but democracy in general. . . . Environmental laws became a great experiment in participatory democracy."[32]

As a result of public and political efforts, the skies over cities became noticeably cleaner, and fish and wildlife populations rebounded throughout the country. A 2012 study by the EPA demonstrates just how important these changes were to public health. The Clean Air Act alone prevented an estimated 184,000 premature deaths and saved an astounding $22 trillion in health care costs over a period of forty years. And the benefits of the Clean Water Act were seen in the once-dead Cuyahoga River. In 2012 blue herons and bald eagles nested along the river's banks, and Cuyahoga waters supported sixty species of fish. Rivers in other industrial cities experienced similar regeneration. A disastrous oil spill in 1969 moved a generation to push for environmental reforms that continue to protect people and wildlife today.

CHAPTER THREE

Culture Clashes

By 1980 the struggle for a cleaner environment had created one of the most powerful social movements in American history. Polls showed that 55 percent of Americans supported the accomplishments of the environmental movement. A majority of Americans also backed the laws Congress passed to regulate toxic chemicals, clean up hazardous waste sites, protect endangered species, and reduce air and water pollution. The widespread mainstream support fueled the rapid growth of environmental groups including the Sierra Club, the National Wildlife Federation, the Natural Resources Defense Council, the Environmental Defense Fund, Friends of the Earth, and Greenpeace. These groups, which spent millions of dollars to lobby legislators and fund political campaigns, became so powerful they were referred to by some as Big Green.

With millions of dollars in donations pouring in, Big Green set up lobbying and research organizations in Washington, DC. In 1986 the National Audubon Society had two hundred paid staffers, while the National Wildlife Federation had five hundred people working to advance a strong environmental agenda. The groups moved into expensive Washington, DC, office buildings and hired bureaucrats to run their operations. Leaders of Big Green groups met regularly to establish consensus on the issues, hold group press conferences, and coordinate their activities. Those who supported this new direction came to be known as mainstream environmentalists.

Powerful Opposition

Many environmentalists were supportive of Big Green's growing power after the first explicitly antienvironmental president was elected in 1980. Republican Ronald Reagan, who served from

1981 to 1989, believed environmental regulations were costly to industry and bad for the economy. Reagan had broad support from corporate polluters who resented what they saw as federal bureaucrats interfering with profitable business practices. One of Reagan's most famous applause lines took direct aim at inspectors who visited industrial sites to regulate pollution: "The most terrifying words in the English language are: I'm from the government and I'm here to help."[33]

Reagan made other statements that alarmed environmentalists. As a candidate, in September 1980 Reagan claimed that trees caused air pollution: "Approximately 80 percent of our air pollution stems from hydrocarbons released by vegetation. So let's not go overboard in setting and enforcing tough emission standards for man-made sources."[34] While Reagan was glibly signaling to supporters that he wished to relax Clean Air Act standards, the statement was wrong on two counts. Hydrocarbons are produced by burning fossil fuels. And trees and other vegetation actually clean the air by absorbing hydrocarbons and other toxic gases like nitrogen oxide and sulfur dioxide. Whatever the factual basis of his statements, Reagan's strategy proved effective, as journalist Thomas Friedman explains: "Reagan ran not only against government in general but against environmental regulation in particular. He . . . turned environmental regulation into a much more partisan and polarizing issue than it had ever been before. It has been so ever since."[35]

> "The most terrifying words in the English language are: I'm from the government and I'm here to help."[33]
>
> —Ronald Reagan, fortieth president of the United States

Reagan made two controversial appointments to powerful agencies that enacted antienvironmental policies. James G. Watt was named secretary of the US Department of the Interior in 1981. Watt was a lawyer and president of the Mountain States Legal Foundation who once called environmentalism a left-wing cult intent on destroying America. The Interior Department controls 500 million acres (202 million ha) of federal lands, equal to

During the 1980s, the aims of environmental groups often conflicted with the beliefs of President Ronald Reagan. A champion of American industry, Reagan appointed several key government officeholders who viewed environmental laws as harmful to the growth of the economy.

20 percent of all US territory. Although the department manages wildlife refuges and recreational areas, including the national parks system, the agency also leases land to private entities for mining, oil and gas drilling, ranching, and logging.

Environmentalists believed the Interior Department should favor the public interest and support conservation and preservation of federal areas. Watt had different ideas, as political journalist Jeffrey St. Clair explains:

> Within a matter of months, Watt proposed the sale of 30 million acres of public lands to private companies, gave away billions of dollars' worth of publicly owned coal resources, fought to permit corporations to manage national parks, refused to enforce the nation's strip mining laws, offered up [offshore] oil reserves to exploration and drilling, ignored the Endangered Species Act, and purged the Interior Department of any employee who objected to his agenda.[36]

The Endangered Species Act

The Endangered Species Act of 1973 is administered by two agencies within the Interior Department: the US Fish and Wildlife Service and the National Marine Fisheries Service. According to a 1978 Supreme Court ruling, the Endangered Species Act was written by Congress to "halt and reverse the trend towards species extinction—whatever the cost." This ruling meant that any project on federal land could not go forward if any species of plant or animal would be endangered (in danger of extinction) or threatened (likely to become endangered).

The federal agencies overseeing the Endangered Species Act can directly list a species as threatened or endangered. Additionally, individuals and environmental organizations can petition the agencies to list a species. When a species is listed, economic factors cannot be considered when protecting ecosystems on which the species depends. That means millions of acres can be set aside to protect an endangered species like the northern spotted owl. The Endangered Species Act has saved many plants and animals from extinction, including the bald eagle, whooping crane, gray wolf, gray whale, grizzly bear, and sea otter. However, antienvironmentalists have long blamed the act for locking up millions of acres of public land while destroying the livelihoods of loggers, ranchers, miners, fishers, and other workers. The Endangered Species Act has generated countless court cases over the years and continues to divide public opinion more than four decades after President Richard Nixon signed the bill into law.

Quoted in "*Tennessee Valley Authority v. Hill*," Public.Resource.org, November 24, 2015. https://law.resource.org.

Reagan's EPA director was equally controversial. Anne M. Gorsuch was an antienvironmental crusader who believed the federal government placed too many restraints on businesses. When Gorsuch took over the EPA, her top advisers were lawyers who previously worked for polluting industries that produced cars, oil, and chemicals. Gorsuch cut the EPA's budget by 22 percent and laid off thirty-two hundred people, 30 percent of the agency's staff. She held secret meetings with industry representatives, relaxed standards in the Clean Air Act, approved the use of previously restricted pesticides, and waived fines against polluters.

Creating an Antienvironmental Movement

With Reagan in the White House, bipartisan support for environmental issues came to an end. In general, Democrats continued to support more stringent laws to protect the environment, while Republicans opposed them. The Republican view was especially strong in western states, where economic growth had long depended on the development of natural resources. In the 1980s logging was a major industry in Idaho, Oregon, and Washington. Coal, oil, and minerals were important to the economies of Wyoming, Utah, Nevada, and Montana. And ranchers everywhere depended on unfettered access to cheap grazing land. The situation in the West pitted ranchers, miners, oil workers, loggers, cowhands, truck drivers, and others who worked outdoors against environmentalists, who were seen as elite, liberal, and out of touch with American values.

President Reagan signed an executive order that allowed ranchers to pay a fee to feed their livestock on public lands. The measure had wide support in Western states where cattle interests and land developers often painted resistant environmental groups as anti-American.

Though there has always been a clash of cultures between urban and rural residents, some of the biggest, most polluting corporations in the world took advantage of the situation to create an antienvironmental movement that continues to exert a powerful political influence today. Companies such as Exxon (now Exxon-Mobil), Chevron, General Motors, Ford, General Electric, Dow, and DuPont deliberately concealed their antienvironmental strategies from voters who would not support the political goals of businesses that profited from pollution. The corporations spent millions to promote their antienvironmental agendas through trade groups such as the Farm Bureau, the American Petroleum Institute, and the American Mining Congress. These organizations lobbied politicians and filed lawsuits to reverse environmental regulations. This led to the rise of associations such as the Mountain States Legal Foundation, which describes itself today as the litigation arm of the antienvironmental movement. Investigative journalist Samantha Sanchez explains how the industry front groups worked:

"[Antienvironmental groups] specialize in rallies, petition drives, even T-shirt and bumper-sticker campaigns—anything that puts a working-man's face on the developers' profit motive."[37]

—Samantha Sanchez, investigative journalist

Although [the antienvironmental] groups typically rely on donations from resource companies and developers, they specialize in rallies, petition drives, even T-shirt and bumper-sticker campaigns—anything that puts a workingman's face on the developers' profit motive. With innocuous, populist-sounding names, these organizations appeal directly to the economic frustration of blue-collar voters.[37]

The Rise of Wise Use

Around three hundred antienvironmental grassroots groups formed during the Reagan era. One of the most influential, the

Center for the Defense of Free Enterprise (CDFE), was founded in Bellevue, Washington, by businessman Alan Gottlieb. Although small donations from average citizens funded some CDFE activities, financial records show that the group was largely funded by lumber giants Georgia-Pacific, Boise Cascade, and Pacific Lumber, along with DuPont and Exxon. In a 1988 speech to the Ontario Forest Industries Association trade group, CDFE vice president Ron Arnold explained why companies should fund antienvironmental front groups:

> Pro-industry citizen activist groups can do things the industry can't. [A front group] can form coalitions to build real political clout. It can be an effective and convincing advocate for your industry. It can evoke powerful archetypes such as the sanctity of the family, the virtue of the close-knit community, the natural wisdom of the rural dweller, and many others I'm sure you can think of. It can use the tactic of the intelligent attack against environmentalists and take the battle to them instead of forever responding to environmentalist initiatives. And it can turn the public against your enemies.[38]

Arnold was a former member of the Sierra Club who became disillusioned when the organization changed its focus from outdoor recreation to environmental activism. Arnold claimed that he stole the organizational manual from the Sierra Club and used it as a guide to build the CDFE into a multimillion-dollar organization with more than thirty thousand members. Arnold is known for using the rhetoric of war in publications and interviews. In his 1987 book *Ecology Wars*, he wrote: "Our goal is to destroy, to eradicate the environmental movement. We're mad as hell. We're not going to take it anymore. We're dead serious—we're going to destroy them. Environmentalism is the

> "Our goal is to destroy, to eradicate the environmental movement. . . . Environmentalism is the new paganism. Trees are worshipped and humans sacrificed at its altar. It is evil."[39]
>
> —Ron Arnold, vice president, CDFE

new paganism. Trees are worshipped and humans sacrificed at its altar. It is evil."[39]

In 1988 Arnold put his words into action when the CDFE cosponsored what was called the Multi-Use Strategy Conference in Reno, Nevada. This pivotal antienvironmental convention was attended by more than three hundred people from sixty different industries. Attendees included representatives from the big trade groups that represented the extractive industries, along with off-road vehicle makers such as Yamaha and the gun rights group the National Rifle Association. After the conference a booklet was published with a twenty-five-point Wise Use agenda that included demands for more logging, drilling, and mining and less protection for endangered species. The agenda was the founding document of the Wise Use movement, which fueled widespread antienvironmentalism throughout the West in the 1990s.

A Bitter Brown Owl Quarrel

As the Wise Use movement gained momentum, its leaders found a perfect symbol to rally blue-collar voters—the northern spotted owl. The US Fish and Wildlife Service, part of the Interior Department, listed the owl as threatened under the Endangered Species Act in 1980. This meant the northern spotted owl was likely to become an endangered species if logging continued on federal lands. Efforts to save the owl fueled one of the most contentious battles of the era.

The northern spotted owl is brown with small white spots. Its habitat is in the lush old-growth forests of the Pacific Northwest. The owl roosts high in large-diameter trees that are from 350 to 750 years old while avoiding clear-cut areas where loggers have removed all the trees. A breeding pair of owls requires at least 2,000 acres (809 ha) to thrive.

Scientists feared that the northern spotted owl was dying off due to widespread logging of old-growth forests in Oregon and Washington. By listing the northern spotted owl as threatened, environmentalists hoped to protect this entire irreplaceable ecosystem that had evolved over millennia. The efforts by environmentalists prevented the timber industry from logging old-growth forests wherever northern spotted owl nests were found.

Under the Endangered Species Act of 1980, the northern spotted owl (shown) was classified as "threatened," which helped environmentalists successfully prevent timber interests from logging the old-growth forests of Washington and Oregon where the owl lived.

> "For the timber industry, long accustomed to clear-cutting in federal forests, [a tree] was a commodity, a renewable resource to be cut down, regrown and cut down again."[40]
>
> —Jonathan Raban, journalist

By 1990 more than two-thirds of the Pacific Northwest's original old-growth forests had already been logged. Of the old-growth forest that remained, 60 percent was located in national forests and available for timber production. To environmentalists, the northern spotted owl symbolized the struggle to protect the earth's dwindling natural resources. To the logging industry, the owl represented government overreach and an irrational barrier to economic development. The timber industry vehemently opposed the decision to list the owl as threatened and predicted dire economic consequences. As journalist Jonathan Raban explains:

> For the timber industry, long accustomed to clear-cutting in federal forests, [a tree] was a commodity, a renewable resource to be cut down, regrown and cut down again. There was no reconciling [with environmentalists]. On one side, the forest primeval, the murmuring pines and the hemlocks, the inviolate wilderness; on the other, people and their histories and traditions, jobs, communities, an economy based entirely on timber.[40]

With the battle lines drawn, industry-funded antienvironmental groups went to work. The complex environmental issue was framed in a simple term: jobs versus owls. However, the issue was far more complex than a bumper sticker slogan. By the 1990s at least one-third of the trees harvested in the Pacific Northwest were exported to Asia for a few dollars per log. And automation was replacing the workers who felled trees and worked in sawmills. These changes in the industry resulted in widespread unemployment in towns that depended on logging. So, even as rural workers blamed the northern spotted owl and environmentalists for their problems, they were more likely victims of globalization and automation.

Anger on Both Sides

Whatever the complex economic forces at work, "Save a logger, eat an owl" was a popular slogan in logging towns throughout the Pacific Northwest. Some local restaurants even served what they claimed was spotted owl barbeque, with ads that read "Spotted Owl Tastes Just like Chicken."[41] Newspapers in the region showed photos of spotted owls shot and nailed to trees. And as the controversy dragged through the courts, the rhetoric against the environmental movement became more heated. Industry-backed groups coordinated angry demonstrations in small towns and organized fax and phone campaigns against environmentalists and their political allies.

The Wise Use movement and the spotted owl controversy powered the growth of the radical environmental group Earth First!. The group, founded in 1980, focused on acts of civil disobedience and minor vandalism to prevent logging. For example, Earth First! organized tree-sitting demonstrations. Protesters occupied platforms built high in tree branches to halt logging operations. Although tree-sitting protests lasted a day or two and brought media attention, other actions of radical environmentalists were condemned by mainstream green groups. One of these actions, called tree spiking, involved driving large nails or metal rods deep into trees destined for logging. The spikes were meant to cause damage to the chainsaws used by loggers or to the expensive blades used in mills where trees are cut into planks. Spikes also discolored the wood, making it less valuable commercially.

A Divided Country

The spotted owl controversy was resolved in 1993 when President Bill Clinton hosted a "timber summit" in Portland, Oregon. The president listened to the grievances of timber workers and heard from environmentalists and scientists. In 1994 Clinton signed the Northwest Forest Plan, which protected around 20 million acres (8 million ha) of federal land from logging. The plan included financial compensation and job retraining programs for unemployed timber workers.

After the owl controversy died down, the Wise Use movement moved on to other issues. And the environmentalists fought back; the hidden corporate funding sources of the Wise Use movement

Violence Against Environmentalists

The antienvironmental Wise Use movement often used violent rhetoric to arouse public anger against environmentalists. And according to licensed private investigator and author David Helvarg, sometimes the heated rhetoric produced real acts of violence. In his 1994 book, *The War Against the Greens*, Helvarg documented hundreds of cases of harassment and brutal acts against environmental activists that often went unpunished in rural communities where police officers supported the Wise Use movement. As Helvarg told an interviewer in 1995:

> This kind of activity has grown in parallel with an organized anti-environmental backlash in the country. Assaults, arsons, dog killings, rape, bombing, possible homicide and several serious attempts at murder. A lot of the violence takes place in rural and low-income communities where often there's a single resource that provides the livelihood for the community. [In] California, for example, [an] environmental attorney in a logging town, the night of the first pro-logging . . . rally in this town, his office front was shot up and a death threat left on its answering machine. Pat Costner, Toxics Director of Greenpeace, a few days before she was going to release a national report on hazardous waste incinerators, her home of 17 years in Arkansas was burned to the ground. They lifted the roof off the remnants of her building and found the gas can that was used to start the fire. . . . The leadership distances itself from the direct violence . . . but at the same time they speak of a national uprising and a potential civil war.

David Helvarg, "The War Against the Greens," *Living on Earth*, 2017. www.loe.org.

were exposed by investigators working with the Sierra Club and the Natural Resources Defense Council. In 1995 the environmental organizations orchestrated a letter-writing campaign that generated more than a million letters to Congress questioning the funding and practices of Wise Use front groups.

Some representatives denounced the Wise Use movement. But the tactics pioneered by the antienvironmental groups continue to divide the country. Today voters in big cities and suburbs tend to support the environmental movement—and vote for Democratic politicians—while voters in rural areas are almost entirely represented by Republicans who oppose most environmental regulations. The struggle to preserve the environment created a rift between people in the city and those in the countryside that has spanned generations and engulfed millions of acres of federal land that belong to all Americans, whatever their political beliefs.

CHAPTER FOUR

New Commitments on Climate Change

In 1988 rain stopped falling throughout much of the United States, and temperatures climbed to record levels from California to North Carolina. The three warmest years on record had already occurred during the 1980s, and 1988 was due to become the hottest year to date.

On June 23, 1988, a Senate hearing on climate change was scheduled in Washington, DC. Coincidentally, the temperature that day surged to a record high of 98°F (36.7°C), and the heat overwhelmed the air conditioner in the Senate hearing room. Senators mopped sweat from their brows as they listened to James Hansen, a climate scientist and the director of the National Aeronautics and Space Administration's (NASA) Goddard Institute for Space Studies. Hansen told the Senate Committee on Energy and Natural Resources that there was a 99 percent certainty that anthropogenic (human-made) climate change was rapidly heating the planet. He explained that carbon dioxide (CO_2), produced by burning coal, oil, and gas, was causing what he referred to as global warming and the greenhouse effect. Hansen predicted that humanity could expect more record-breaking temperatures, extended droughts, and severe storms in the future. When reporters surrounded Hansen after the hearings, he warned, "It's time to stop waffling so much and say that the greenhouse effect is here and affecting our climate now."[42]

This was not the first time Hansen connected human activities to climate change. In 1982 he appeared at a hearing in the

House of Representatives organized by Al Gore, who was then a Tennessee representative. Gore assumed that when Hansen explained the greenhouse effect to other members of Congress, they would be alarmed. But Gore discovered that his colleagues were either uninterested or did not believe that rising CO_2 levels presented a problem.

A Worldwide Problem

By 1988 Gore was a senator, and the American public was starting to pay attention to the issue. That year 58 percent of Americans said they had heard of or read about global warming, a 20 percent increase since 1982. The growing awareness of climate change galvanized the environmental community. On April 22, 1990, the twentieth anniversary of Earth Day was celebrated by 200 million people in 141 countries. One of the largest demonstrations was held in Washington, DC, where politicians and some of the biggest celebrities of the day gave speeches about climate change and other topics. Gaylord Nelson, who had organized the first Earth Day, gave a speech in which he reminded environmentalists that they had an obligation to future generations: "I don't want to come back here 20 years from now and have to tell your sons and daughters that you didn't do your duty."[43]

> "I don't want to come back here 20 years from now and have to tell your sons and daughters that you didn't do your duty."[43]
>
> —Gaylord Nelson, Earth Day organizer

Soon after Earth Day, Nelson's words took on even greater importance when the United Nations Intergovernmental Panel on Climate Change (IPCC) released conclusions from a two-year study. The IPCC, which remains active today, is composed of twenty-five hundred experts from more than sixty countries who work in widely divergent fields such as climatology, ecology, economics, medicine, and oceanography. Because of this wide range of expertise, the IPCC has been viewed by scientists and environmentalists as the most credible organization studying

A flag of the planet waves over a crowd in front of the US Capitol on April 22, 1990. Over 100,000 people attended celebrations at the nation's capital on that day, the twentieth anniversary of the first Earth Day.

global warming. The 1990 IPCC report stated, "We are certain that emissions resulting from human activities are substantially increasing the atmospheric concentrations of the greenhouse gases: carbon dioxide, methane . . . and nitrous oxide. These increases will enhance the greenhouse effect, resulting on average in an additional warming of the Earth's surface."[44]

The IPCC report paved the way for the groundbreaking 1992 United Nations Earth Summit in Rio de Janeiro, Brazil. The twelve-day Earth Summit was the first international conference to address global climate change. The summit was attended by seventeen thousand people, including heads of state from 102 countries. In addition to government representatives and climate experts, the Earth Summit drew grassroots environmental groups that represented children, women, and indigenous people from around the world. It was one of the first times environmental groups based in developing nations publicly expressed concern over climate change and other green issues.

Delegates at the Earth Summit produced the Framework Convention on Climate Change (FCCC), a treaty signed by government leaders in 154 countries. The FCCC stated that industrial nations should take immediate steps to reduce global warming emissions. However, the framework was completely voluntary. Signatories did not have to set specific goals, there was no time frame set for reducing emissions, and no penalties were proposed for nations that did not follow the FCCC recommendations.

Denying Global Warming

In November 1992, less than six months after the Earth Summit, Democrat Bill Clinton was elected president. While Clinton was not known as a committed environmentalist, Gore was his vice president. Gore persuaded the Clinton administration to endorse a US "Climate Change Action Plan" that formally committed the United States to reducing greenhouse gas emissions. However, the powerful antienvironmental forces that sponsored the Wise Use movement in the West were also working to challenge the science behind climate change. Oil companies, automakers, and coal producers sponsored numerous front groups with names like the Global Climate Coalition and the Global Climate Information Project. These groups spent tens of millions of dollars to raise uncertainties about climate change while providing huge campaign contributions to Democratic and Republican politicians alike. As physicist Spencer Weart explains, "Right-leaning think tanks redoubled their efforts to deny that global warming posed a threat. . . . A typical argument in the pamphlets, op-ed essays, and press conferences was to point with horror at the specter of a tax on [carbon] emissions. They claimed it would impose a dreadful rise in gasoline prices, supposedly intolerable to Americans."[45]

> "Right-leaning think tanks redoubled their efforts to deny that global warming posed a threat."[45]
>
> —Spencer Weart, physicist

Gore ran for president in 2000 but narrowly lost to George W. Bush, a Texas Republican and former oilman. The Bush administration followed the same antienvironmental strategies first used by Ronald Reagan in the 1980s. Bush chose antienvironmentalists to head the Interior Department, the EPA, and other agencies. Important positions were filled by pro-industry lobbyists. By the time Bush was elected to a second term in 2004, he had rolled back more than two hundred environmental laws, weakening protection of the country's air, water, public lands, and wildlife. Although these policies were popular with big business, Bush understood that most Americans supported the goals of the environmental movement.

To make his antienvironmental policies more palatable to the public, Bush hired pollster Frank Luntz to conduct focus groups with average Americans about environmental issues. Luntz concluded, "The environment is probably the single issue on which Republicans in general and President Bush in particular are most [politically] vulnerable. . . . [The public views Republicans as being] in the pockets of corporate fat cats who rub their hands together and chuckle maniacally as they plot to pollute America for fun and profit."[46]

Luntz advised Bush to use the rhetoric of the environmental movement while dismantling environmental laws. Bush followed this advice when he called his initiative to repeal key provisions of the Clean Air Act the Clear Skies Act. He called his plan to increase logging of old-growth forests the Healthy Forests Restoration Act. The Bush administration also worked to alter, suppress, or discredit more than twenty reports on climate change, including a ten-year study by the IPCC released in 2003 that stated the effects of climate change were going to be far worse than first believed.

Shining a Light on Climate Change

The threat of climate change helped make Gore a leading voice in the environmental movement. In speeches, Gore often repeated a line from his 1992 book, *Earth in the Balance*: "We must make

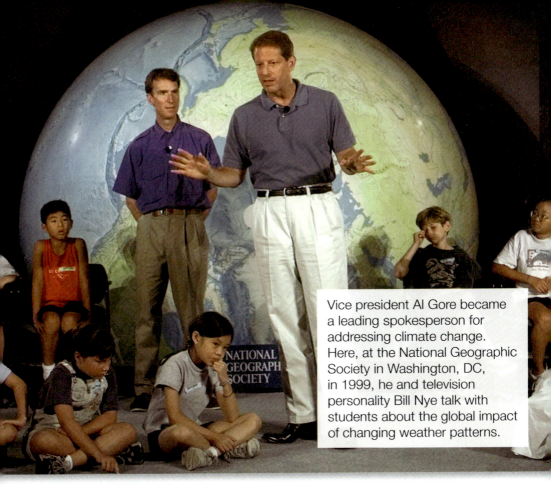

Vice president Al Gore became a leading spokesperson for addressing climate change. Here, at the National Geographic Society in Washington, DC, in 1999, he and television personality Bill Nye talk with students about the global impact of changing weather patterns.

the rescue of the environment the central organizing principle for civilization."[47] In the early 2000s Gore did his part to rescue the environment through educational efforts. He put together a slide show presentation that explained what he called the "planetary emergency"[48] of climate change. Gore narrated the presentation, which mixed shocking photographs of environmental disasters with maps, bullet points, graphs, and flip charts. The presentation connected climate change to drought patterns, animal extinctions, destructive rain and snowstorms, melting polar ice sheets, and other problems caused by the warming planet. Gore estimates that over the years, he presented his slide show more than one thousand times at environmental conferences, political gatherings, and community events.

In 2004 environmental activist Laurie David saw a ten-minute version of Gore's slide show in Los Angeles. In 2016

David recalled her reaction: "My jaw dropped. I had been killing myself trying to find the language to explain this issue to people in a way that they could digest. Here Al Gore had it. I was just floored."[49] David, a prominent member of the Natural Resources Defense Council, was married to Larry David, a wealthy television producer. Laurie David drew on her Hollywood connections to turn Gore's slide show into the full-length film *An Inconvenient Truth*. The 2006 film explained the science of climate change in easily understandable terms that helped raise international public awareness about the issue.

An Inconvenient Truth went on to become the third-highest-grossing documentary of all time and won an Academy Award for Best Documentary. When Gore accepted the award, he told

A Life-Changing Film

The 2006 film *An Inconvenient Truth* helped make Al Gore the face of the environmental movement. Some students who saw the film described it as a wake-up call that changed the course of their lives. On the tenth anniversary of the film's release, the Climate Reality Project, founded by Gore, asked people who were students in 2006 to share stories about the impact *An Inconvenient Truth* had on their lives. Taylor Fiscus said she went into politics after seeing the film and worked on environmental policy, first in the White House and later at the EPA. Andy Oury said *An Inconvenient Truth* inspired him to become an engineer who designs batteries for hybrid and electric cars. Sandip Chowdhury, who resides in India, explained the influence of *An Inconvenient Truth* on his life:

> I am not exaggerating when I say that the documentary was a turning point in my life. Not only did it expose me to the reality of climate change but also it gave me purpose. . . . [I] studied forestry and environment management for two years in [India and] I am right here fighting for our planet and living the dream. Thanks to *An Inconvenient Truth*, I have found meaning and purpose in my life.

Quoted in Climate Reality Project, "Four Ways *An Inconvenient Truth* Changed Peoples' Lives," May 27, 2016. www.climaterealityproject.org.

the audience, "My fellow Americans, people all over the world, we need to solve the climate crisis. It's not a political issue; it's a moral issue. We have everything we need to get started, with the possible exception of the will to act. That's a renewable resource. Let's renew it."[50]

Obama Appoints Environmentalists

An Inconvenient Truth put the issue of climate change on the political agenda. During the 2008 presidential campaign, candidate John McCain promised action on climate change: "The facts of global warming demand our urgent attention, especially in Washington. Good stewardship, prudence, and simple common sense demand that we act to meet the challenge, and act quickly."[51] McCain was the Republican in the race, which made his statement particularly noteworthy. But McCain lost to Democrat Barack Obama, who often stated

> "We need to solve the climate crisis. It's not a political issue; it's a moral issue."[50]
>
> —Al Gore, forty-fifth vice president of the United States

his belief that the United States should be the world leader in protecting the environment and combating climate change.

Obama was elected during a time of extreme financial turmoil known as the Great Recession. During his first years in office, his administration focused on the economy while working on a law to provide health care to millions of Americans. But Obama also shifted away from the antienvironmental policies of the Bush administration. He appointed nearly forty influential environmentalists to the White House staff, the EPA, and the US Departments of Agriculture, Commerce, Energy, and the Interior. Lisa Jackson, an advocate for clean energy and regulating carbon emissions, was appointed to run the EPA. David Hayes, a former fellow at the World Wildlife Fund, took over as the deputy secretary of the interior, the number two job in the department. Cathy Zoi, assistant secretary for Energy Efficiency and Renewable Energy at the US Department of Energy, was a former chief executive officer of the

Alliance for Climate Protection. Obama's top energy and environment adviser, Carol Browner, was a former head of the National Audubon Society.

After Obama was reelected in 2012, he made a historic commitment to combating climate change. As the president stated in his second inaugural address in 2013:

> We will respond to the threat of climate change, knowing that the failure to do so would betray our children and future generations. . . . The path towards sustainable energy sources will be long and sometimes difficult. But America cannot resist this transition, we must lead it. We cannot cede to other nations the technology that will power new jobs and new industries, we must claim its promise.[52]

The Environmental President

Most of Obama's policies were opposed by Republicans in Congress, who refused to consider any new environmental legislation the president proposed. Obama went around congressional obstruction by issuing executive orders that directed government agencies to institute environmental policies. Unlike laws passed by Congress, executive orders are not permanent; they can be repealed or withdrawn by future presidents.

Obama's most far-reaching executive order was the President's Climate Action Plan of 2013. The plan established carbon pollution standards for power plants, which are the largest emitters of CO_2 in the United States. Other provisions of the Climate Action Plan were aimed at increasing gas mileage in new cars, protecting the nation's air and water from pollution, reducing toxic substance production, and cutting energy waste.

"We will respond to the threat of climate change, knowing that the failure to do so would betray our children and future generations."[52]

—Barack Obama, forty-fourth president of the United States

Obama took other actions that were not specifically focused on climate change but would help improve the overall environment. For example, the president created the largest marine reserve in the world by expanding the Pacific Remote Islands Marine National Monument to encompass 490,000 square miles (1.27 million sq. km). The reserve protects corals, fish, shellfish, birds, insects, and plants from oil and mineral extraction and all commercial fishing. Obama also used his authority under a 1906 law called the Antiquities Act to create twenty-six national monuments in New Mexico, Utah, Nevada, California, and elsewhere. Additionally, Obama added 465 million acres (188 million ha) to existing national monuments. In doing so, the president designated more land, by hundreds of millions of acres, than any of his predecessors.

The Kingman Reef includes a small atoll and twelve miles of submerged coral lying between the Hawaiian Islands and American Samoa. In 2009, President George W. Bush preserved the reef and six nearby islands as parts of the Pacific Remote Islands Marine National Monument.

The Fracking Divide

Despite Obama's having one of the best environmental records of any president, some of his policies were criticized by environmentalists. During both his election campaigns, Obama took large contributions from oil and gas companies that were involved in the controversial practice known as hydraulic fracturing, or fracking. The fracking process is used to extract oil and gas located deep underground between layers of shale. Oil companies use massive quantities of water containing highly toxic chemicals while fracking. This process has been blamed for polluting groundwater in Pennsylvania, New York, Ohio, Texas, Wyoming, and elsewhere.

Fracking is widely used to extract natural gas, which creates 47 percent less CO_2 than coal when used in power plants. Because natural gas power plants have lower emissions, Obama supported the fracking boom that was occurring throughout the United States. The president believed that natural gas could act as a "bridge" between coal power and solar, wind, and other renewable energy sources. (The concept of a bridge fuel originated with the American Gas Association trade group in the 1980s.) Environmentalists were unhappy when Obama explained this view in his 2014 State of the Union address: "If extracted safely natural gas is the 'bridge fuel' that can power our economy with less of the carbon pollution that causes climate change."[53]

Environmentalists point out that the United States cannot drastically lower carbon emissions if hundreds of new natural gas power plants are built. While the Obama administration envisioned using natural gas–burning power plants until 2050, environmentalists call the fuel a bridge to nowhere. They point out that natural gas is mostly methane, which is also a potent climate change gas. The nation's natural gas infrastructure leaks a significant amount of methane into the atmosphere. As environmental journalist Brad Plumer comments, "Natural gas makes most sense as a bridge if we're willing to chance a hefty dose of global warming—with all the risks that come with it, from rising sea levels, to droughts to withering food production."[54]

The President's Climate Action Plan

In 2013 President Barack Obama issued an executive order called the President's Climate Action Plan. The plan instituted tough new rules to reduce carbon pollution from power plants by 2030 to a level 32 percent below 2005 levels. According to the EPA, that policy would keep 870 million tons (789 million metric tons) of carbon pollution out of the atmosphere. That amount is equal to the annual emissions from 70 percent of the nation's passenger vehicles. The Climate Action Plan also ordered automakers to double fuel economy for medium-sized vehicles and trucks by 2025. New energy-efficiency standards for appliances and electrical equipment were put in place to reduce energy waste. The executive order also contained proposals to expand the clean energy economy by increasing the number of renewable energy projects on federal lands.

The Climate Action Plan was very popular; a 2013 NBC/*Wall Street Journal* poll showed that two-thirds of voters backed strong curbs on coal-plant emissions. More than half said they would even accept higher electricity bills to implement those curbs. Former New Mexico senator Jeff Bingaman explained the popularity of Obama's policies: "He's in sync with the American public in making this a priority. I think we're getting more and more to a point where a politician or an officeholder who's opposed to doing anything for dealing with this problem is somewhat on the defensive."

Quoted in Darren Samuelsohn, "The Greening of Barack Obama," *Politico*, November 18, 2014. www.politico.com.

A Political Football

Whatever the policy differences, it was clear that climate change had become a political football, an issue kicked back and forth between opposing parties. Public opinion about climate change is also strongly divided along ideological lines. According to a 2015 poll by the Pew Research Center, 71 percent of Democrats say the earth is warming primarily due to human activity. Only 27 percent of Republicans agree with that view. These opinions differ from multiple studies published in scientific journals that show that at least 97 percent of climate scientists say warming trends over the past century are unquestionably due to human activities. While most in the environmental movement agree with climate scientists, the battle took on greater urgency after Obama's presidency came to an end in 2017.

CHAPTER FIVE

New Leaders Continue the Battle

In 2014 the fifth report by the IPCC was released. The five-thousand-page assessment reinforced statements made in previous reports since 1990, but the tone was more dire than ever. The IPCC reiterated that humans are causing climate change but used dramatic language to predict a "very high risk of severe, widespread, and irreversible impacts globally by 2100."[55] Irreversible impacts include melting of the West Antarctic Ice Sheet, a 10- to 13-foot (3 to 4 m) rise in sea levels, and the widespread extinction of numerous plants and animals. As United Nations secretary-general Ban Ki-moon told reporters, "Science has spoken. There is no ambiguity in their message. Leaders must act; time is not on our side."[56]

Ban's message was particularly relevant to young environmentalists who were born into a world with a changing climate. As twenty-three-year-old environmental activist Daisy Kendrick writes, "The news should be a starting gun for a new wave of activism, action and change. Because . . . the real change is going to come from us. Call us millennials or Gen Z or Net Gen, we're the consumers, employees, employers and future leaders who will see the devastating effects of climate change."[57]

The IPCC report also made clear that negative effects of a warming world will hit the poor and communities of color with greater force. As Hispanic lawyer Alfredo Padilla explains, "It's obviously happening, the flooding, the record droughts. . . . And all this affects poor people harder. Their jobs are more based on weather. And when there are hurricanes, when there is flooding, who gets hit the worst? The people on the poor side of town."[58]

Padilla is not alone in his concerns. A 2015 *New York Times* poll showed that Hispanics are far more likely than whites to view climate change as a problem that affects them personally. According to the poll, 54 percent of Hispanics rated global warming as very important to them personally, compared with 37 percent of white respondents. And 63 percent of Hispanics said the federal government should act broadly to address global warming, compared with 49 percent of whites. African Americans also strongly back climate action, with 83 percent supporting limits on carbon pollution.

> **"When there are hurricanes, when there is flooding, who gets hit the worst? The people on the poor side of town."[58]**
>
> —Alfredo Padilla, lawyer

Native Americans Fight for Clean Water

No communities are more threatened by climate change than those of Native Americans. That is the message of Indigenous Environmental Network founder Tom Goldtooth, who says, "Populations such as ours that have a close relationship with nature . . . are experiencing these real effects, from Alaska to many of our tribal people here in the lower 48 [states]. Climate change is real. It's not, as some believe, just some conspiracy theory."[59]

Tom and his son Dallas Goldtooth were prominent organizers of the Dakota Access Pipeline protests that made headlines in 2016. The grassroots protest movement tried to prevent construction of a $3.7 billion crude oil pipeline in western North Dakota. The pipeline would pass under the Missouri River less than 1 mile (1.6 km) from the Standing Rock Indian Reservation, home to the Standing Rock Sioux Tribe.

The Native American protesters wanted to stop the Dakota Access Pipeline for several reasons. Many believe the best way to slow climate change is to keep oil in the ground so that it will not be burned. The Dakota Access Pipeline would make crude oil easier to transport, which would encourage more oil production, thus contributing to climate change. There were also fears

Heavy equipment buries sections of an oil pipeline near Native American land in North Dakota. The Standing Rock Sioux turned out in 2016 to resist the building of the pipeline, which edged close to waterways that the tribe feared might become polluted if a spill were to occur.

that the pipeline would leak into the Missouri and contaminate the reservation's only freshwater supply. The Dakota Access Pipeline was originally planned to cross under the river near the state capital of Bismarck, but the project was deemed too risky to local water supplies. Relocation to an area closer to the reservation struck opponents as a clear case of bias.

In April 2016 Standing Rock Sioux tribal members LaDonna Brave Bull Allard and her grandchildren set up Sacred Stone Camp on private land near the pipeline construction site. By the end of the month, Native Americans from an estimated three hundred tribes throughout the country had come to protest, creating the largest gathering of tribes in a century. By the summer the demonstration had attracted an estimated thirty-five hundred pipeline protesters of all races and backgrounds to North Dakota.

Hundreds more, including celebrities such as Leonardo DiCaprio, filled out the crowd on weekends and holidays.

Uniting Generations

As the protests intensified, thirty young Standing Rock Sioux formed a group called Rezpect Our Water (*Rez* is slang for reservation). The group collected stories by young people who described how they would be impacted if the pipeline leaked. Members of Rezpect Our Water collected 140,000 signatures on a petition to stop the pipeline and organized a relay race to deliver the petition to President Barack Obama in Washington, DC. In August 2016 the three-week, 2,000-mile (3,219 km) run from North Dakota culminated with dozens of young Native Americans singing, drumming, and marching in front of the White House. Jasilyn Charger of the Cheyenne River Sioux addressed the protesters, saying, "It's up to us to hold our government accountable. Our land is in danger, as well as our identity, but we will not stand in silence. We are . . . uniting [Indian] nations that have been separate for generations. We must take advantage of this chance to make a change."[60]

> "Our land is in danger, as well as our identity, but we will not stand in silence. . . . We must take advantage of this chance to make a change."[60]
>
> —Jasilyn Charger, Native American activist

In early September, Standing Rock protesters attempted to halt construction by locking themselves to heavy construction equipment. The company building the pipeline, Energy Transfer Partners, brought in private security guards, who used pepper spray and attack dogs to roust the protesters. By October, North Dakota authorities were using harsher methods to harass protesters, including Tasers, pepper spray, concussion grenades, and high-pitched sound cannons. Those who were arrested were held in dog kennels and subjected to freezing temperatures. On one frigid day, authorities turned fire hoses on protesters, spraying them with freezing water.

When the harsh North Dakota winter set in, the number of protesters dwindled. But in December over four thousand US military veterans joined in the opposition. The group Veterans Stand for Standing Rock braved subzero temperatures to show solidarity with the protesters. However, the protest ultimately failed—construction on the pipeline resumed in 2017.

Wake Up and Face the Challenges

As one of the largest grassroots environmental protests in recent history was making headlines, one of the most antienvironmentalist candidates in history was running for president. Republican Donald Trump campaigned on the notion that climate change was a hoax invented by the Chinese to destroy the American economy. In campaign speeches, Trump often stated the environmental

In 2017 many Americans took to the streets to protest President Donald Trump's decision to withdraw the United States form the Paris climate accord. To environmentalists, the accord signifies a global commitment to respond to the perils of human-influenced climate change.

movement "was out of control."[61] He pledged to gut environmental regulations and roll back Obama's executive orders meant to slow climate change.

On November 9, 2016, Trump was elected the forty-fifth president of the United States. When seventeen-year-old indigenous environmental activist Xiuhtezcatl (pronounced "Shoe-TEZ-cahtl") Martinez learned of Trump's victory, he said he felt as if ice water had been dumped on his head—but he also found hope: "The feeling sucked but I knew it could wake us up. For many of us who care about . . . climate change, it was shocking. The feeling was awful, but I think something this alarming is necessary to wake people up and get them to face the challenges we can no longer wait to address."[62]

Martinez is the youth director of the conservation organization Earth Guardians. The organization, founded in 1992 by Martinez's mother, Tamara Rose, is made up of activists, artists, and musicians. Today Earth Guardians is part of a global youth movement working to organize and inspire the next generation of environmentalists. In 2015 Martinez addressed the United Nations General Assembly on climate change, the youngest person ever to do so. As his fame grew, Martinez appeared on numerous television programs, including *The Daily Show* and *Real Time with Bill Maher*.

Suing the Federal Government

In 2015 Earth Guardians joined with the activist group Our Children's Trust to sue the US government over climate change. A total of twenty-one litigants, or plaintiffs, filed the lawsuit in US district court in Oregon. The youngest plaintiff, Avery McRae, was nine years old. Twenty-one-year-old Kelsey Cascadia Juliana was the oldest in the group. As lead plaintiff, her name was attached to the case: *Juliana v. United States*. Juliana explains why she joined the lawsuit: "I believe that climate change is the most pressing issue my generation will ever face, indeed that the world has ever faced. This is an environmental issue and it is also a human rights issue."[63]

The lawsuit is based on a concept called the public trust doctrine, which declares that the government manages the lands, water, fisheries, and other resources for the good of its citizens. The plaintiffs contend that the atmosphere is also part of the public trust. The lawsuit charges the government with deliberately taking actions that worsened the effects of climate change. According to Our Children's Trust, these actions "violated the youngest generation's constitutional rights to life, liberty, and property, as well as failed to protect essential public trust resources."[64]

> "Climate change is the most pressing issue my generation will ever face, indeed that the world has ever faced."[63]
>
> —Kelsey Cascadia Juliana, environmental activist

Juliana v. United States claims that for fifty years the federal government was aware of the climate-damaging effects of rising CO_2 levels but continued to enact policies and practices that promoted the use of fossil fuels. Rather than follow a rational path to phase out carbon-producing fuels, the complaint alleges, the government

> continued to permit, authorize, and subsidize fossil fuel extraction, development, consumption and exportation—activities producing enormous quantities of CO_2 emissions. . . . Through its policies and practices, the Federal Government bears a higher degree of responsibility than any other individual, entity, or country for exposing Plaintiffs to the present dangerous atmospheric CO_2 concentration.[65]

The first hearing for *Juliana v. United States* took place in Eugene, Oregon, in March 2016. The plaintiffs were joined by hundreds of students, activists, and scientists, who crowded into the courtroom. Martinez describes the scene:

> It was amazing to see kids between the ages of 8 and 20 intently listening in on the hearing. We wanted the judge to

see who we were, so he could put a face to this lawsuit. Each kid had their own unique story linking them to climate change. I remember listening to 9-year-old Levi from Florida speak about how rising sea levels are going to wash away his home. Our heartfelt stories were sources of inspiration, as people saw us taking a stand for our future.[66]

When the plaintiffs first filed the case, few legal observers believed their lawsuit would get a hearing; most courts have rejected plaintiffs who try to sue the federal government. Yet despite strong

Indigenous Climate Justice

Xiuhtezcatl Martinez was one of many young indigenous environmental activists who joined in a six-month protest against construction of the Dakota Access Pipeline on the Standing Rock Indian Reservation. Although protesters failed to halt the project, Martinez says the mark of his generation was made. Martinez explains in his autobiography, *We Rise*:

Standing Rock was not just about one pipeline, it symbolized a struggle for justice of all kinds—racial justice, economic justice, treaty justice, gender justice, and climate justice. Those fights were all alive at Standing Rock. It is the latest in a long line of brave actions that cause us to pause and re-examine the true meaning of the word "justice." Like the lunch counter sit-ins of the Civil Rights Movement, Standing Rock made it impossible to ignore the historic and present oppression of indigenous peoples. . . . Climate change is a problem that affects everyone. However, for people who are more reliant on the land, the impacts of floods, droughts, tornadoes, melting ice caps, and other disasters are even worse. The wealthy can pick up and leave or create physical barriers and safeguards to protect against these growing threats, while people without means are forced to reconcile with life as a refugee. For native people, who have a spiritual connection with the land, leaving home can represent an enormous loss of ancestral history. Indigenous rights means climate justice.

Xiuhtezcatl Martinez, *We Rise*. El Segundo, CA: Rodale, 2017, pp. 173–74.

opposition from both the Obama and Trump administrations, the case proceeded through various court hearings. In July 2017 Oregon US district court judge Ann Aiken ruled the case had merit and set a 2018 trial date. The plaintiffs hoped their case would force the government to institute a national Climate Recovery Plan that will significantly reduce CO_2 and other climate-changing gas emissions.

Whatever the merits of the court case, Trump was moving to reverse climate change policies put in place by the Obama administration. In June 2017 Trump announced that the United States would leave the Paris climate accord negotiated by 195 countries in 2015. The agreement was seen as the most promising effort ever taken to tackle climate change. The Paris Agreement committed every member country—including the United States—to drastically reduce greenhouse gas emissions. The United States is responsible for about one-fifth of global carbon emissions. Under the agreement, the United States would be required to cut greenhouse gas emissions to 27 percent below 2005 levels by 2025. The United States would also commit up to $3 billion to help developing nations lower their emissions.

A Stark Choice

By pulling out of the Paris Agreement, Trump signaled that he did not want the US government to address climate change in any way and that he was not interested in participating in future talks about the issue. But if nothing is done about climate change, children born today will live in a drastically different world. According to the 2017 *Climate Science Special Report* prepared by the US government, the middle of the twenty-first century will be marked by massive wildfires, floods, hurricanes, and other disasters. These events will be far more destructive than even the record-setting disasters that occurred in the 2010s.

Despite the bad news, there are those in the environmental movement who remain optimistic, including Al Gore. In the years

Many scientists warn that if climate change continues unaddressed, then future storms, wildfires, floods, and other natural catastrophes might grow in frequency and severity. Some, however, are hopeful that meaningful dialogue between nations can still help avert climatic disaster.

after the 2006 release of *An Inconvenient Truth*, Gore trained a new generation of environmental activists through his Climate Reality Leadership Corps. By 2017 more than ten thousand climate reality leaders in 135 countries had attended Gore's training events. These grassroots organizers teach others about the dangers presented by climate change and encourage participants to demand action from political and business leaders in their own communities.

On the tenth anniversary of *An Inconvenient Truth*, Gore released another film, *An Inconvenient Sequel: Truth to Power*. While the film was not as popular as the original, the release cemented Gore's reputation as a leading voice in the environmental

The *Climate Science Special Report*

In November 2017 an organization called the US Global Change Research Program (USGCRP) released the *Climate Science Special Report*. Thirteen federal agencies participated in the research program, including the EPA, NASA, the National Science Foundation, and the US Departments of Agriculture, Commerce, Defense, Energy, State, and the Interior. The Trump administration could not stop the release of the *Climate Science Special Report*; a law called the Global Change Research Act of 1990 mandates that the federal agencies periodically prepare a report on climate change.

The findings of the *Climate Science Special Report* were clear. According to the USGCRP website, "Climate change is happening now. The United States and the world are warming, global sea level is rising, and some types of extreme weather events are becoming more frequent and more severe. These changes have already resulted in a wide range of impacts across every region of the country and many sectors of the economy."

The report stated that the USGCRP was dedicated to implementing President Barack Obama's 2013 Climate Action Plan to reduce carbon emissions and prepare the nation for the impacts of climate change. However, many members of the Trump administration are climate change deniers. EPA administrator Scott Pruitt has often stated that he does not believe fossil fuels are the main cause of climate change and has moved to repeal key elements of the Climate Action Plan. Pruitt supports Trump's America First Energy Plan, which calls for a massive increase in fracking, coal mining, and offshore oil drilling.

US Global Change Research Program, "Climate Change," 2017. www.globalchange.gov.

movement. While many scenes in *An Inconvenient Sequel* show that climate change is worsening, Gore continues to express hope:

This movement to solve the climate crisis is in the tradition of every great moral movement that has advanced the cause of humankind. And every single one of them has met with resistance to the point where many of the advocates felt despair and wondered, "How long is this gonna take?" How long? Not long. . . . Because of who we are as human beings, the outcome is foreordained. And it is right to save the future for humanity! It is wrong to pollute this Earth and destroy the climate balance! It is right to give hope to the future generation![67]

This message has been guiding the environmental movement since the 1960s. There have been setbacks and great leaps forward. Today old-growth forests that were environmental battlegrounds in decades past attract millions of tourists every year. Even the most ardent antienvironmentalists do not wish to return to an era when rivers burned and hundreds died during temperature inversions. Great gains have been made, and as the original generation of environmentalists passes into history, it will be up to the youngest generation to carry on the work and keep the heritage of the environmental movement alive.

> "It is right to save the future for humanity! It is wrong to pollute this Earth and destroy the climate balance! It is right to give hope to the future generation!"[67]
>
> —Al Gore, forty-fifth vice president of the United States

SOURCE NOTES

Introduction: A Broad-Based Movement

1. Quoted in Carl Safina, *A Sea in Flames: The Deepwater Horizon Oil Blowout*. New York: Crown, 2011, p. 55.
2. Earth Day Network, "The History of Earth Day," 2017. www.earthday.org.
3. Quoted in Nell Greenfield-Boyce, "Trump Picks Oklahoma Attorney General Scott Pruitt to Lead EPA," NPR, December 7, 2016. www.npr.org.
4. Quoted in Monica Anderson, "For Earth Day, Here's How Americans View Environmental Issues," Pew Research Center, April 20, 2017. www.pewresearch.org.

Chapter One: Creating a Movement

5. Rachel Carson, *Silent Spring*. Greenwich, CT: Crest, 1962, p. 10.
6. Carson, *Silent Spring*, p. 10.
7. Quoted in Natural Resources Defense Council, "The Story of Silent Spring," August 13, 2015. www.nrdc.org.
8. Carson, *Silent Spring*, p. 17.
9. Carson, *Silent Spring*, p. 21.
10. Linda Lear, *Rachel Carson: Witness for Nature*. New York: Mariner, 1997, p. 429.
11. Quoted in Johnathan Norton Leonard, "Rachel Carson Dies of Cancer: 'Silent Spring' Author Was 56," *New York Times*, April 15, 1964. www.nytimes.com.
12. H. Patricia Hynes, *The Recurring Silent Spring*. Oxford, UK: Pergamon, 1989, p. 3.
13. Charles Wurster, "DDT Wars and the Birth of the EDF," Environmental Defense Fund, 2015. www.edf.org.
14. Wurster, "DDT Wars and the Birth of the EDF."
15. Wurster, "DDT Wars and the Birth of the EDF."
16. John Wesley Powell, *Canyons of the Colorado*. New York: Cosimo Classics, 2008, p. 237.
17. Quoted in Byron E. Pearson, *Still the Wild River Runs*. Tucson: University of Arizona Press, 2002, p. 54.

18. Sierra Club, "Now Only You Can Save the Grand Canyon from Being Flooded . . . for Profit," *New York Times*, June 9, 1966, p. L35.
19. Quoted in Paul Vitello, "Martin Litton, Fighter for the Environment, Dies at 97," *New York Times*, December 6, 2014. www.nytimes.com.

Chapter Two: Working for Cleaner Air and Water

20. William Wise, *Killer Smog: The World's Worst Air Pollution Disaster*. Chicago: Rand McNally, 1968, p. 14.
21. Quoted in Kate Wheeling and Max Ufberg, "'The Ocean Is Boiling': The Complete Oral History of the 1969 Santa Barbara Oil Spill," *Pacific Standard*, April 18, 2017. https://psmag.com.
22. Quoted in Wheeling and Ufberg, "'The Ocean Is Boiling.'"
23. Quoted Robert Easton, *Black Tide: The Santa Barbara Oil Spill and Its Consequences*. New York: Delacorte, 1972, p. 69.
24. Quoted in Gerhard Peters and John T. Woolley, "Remarks Following Inspection of Oil Damage at Santa Barbara Beach," American Presidency Project, 2017. www.presidency.ucsb.edu.
25. Quoted in Wheeling and Ufberg, "'The Ocean Is Boiling.'"
26. Quoted in Nelson Institute for Environmental Studies, "Gaylord Nelson and Earth Day," 2017. www.nelsonearthday.net.
27. US Department of Energy, "The National Environmental Policy Act of 1969," 2017. https://energy.gov.
28. Quoted in Wheeling and Ufberg, "'The Ocean Is Boiling.'"
29. Quoted in Jim Kershner, "NEPA, the National Environmental Policy," HistoryLink.org, August 27, 2011. www.historylink.org.
30. Meridian International Center, "U.S. Environmental Protection Agency," 2017. www.meridian.org.
31. Quoted in Wheeling and Ufberg, "'The Ocean Is Boiling.'"
32. Cody Ferguson, *This Is Our Land: Grassroots Environmentalism in the Late Twentieth Century*. New Brunswick, NJ: Rutgers University Press, 2015, p. 8.

Chapter Three: Culture Clashes

33. Quoted in Dadlyedly, "The Nine Most Terrifying Words in the English Language," *Daily Kos* (blog), September 24, 2009. www.dailykos.com.
34. Quoted in *New York Times*, "Will Reagan's Luck Outlast Reagan?," January 1, 1989. www.nytimes.com.

35. Thomas Friedman, *Hot, Flat, and Crowded*. New York: Farrar, Straus, and Giroux, 2008, p. 15.
36. Jeffrey St. Clair, "Roaming Charges: Toxic Mom: The Short, Terrible Career of Anne Gorsuch," *CounterPunch*, February 3, 2017. www.counterpunch.org.
37. Samantha Sanchez, "How the West Is Won: Astroturf Lobbying and the 'Wise Use' Movement," *American Prospect*, March–April 1996. http://prospect.org.
38. Quoted in Will Koop, "The Working Forest: 'End of the Commons,'" BC Tap Water Alliance, April 30, 2003. www.bctwa.org.
39. Quoted in K.R. Gupta et al., *Global Environment: Problems and Policies*, vol. 2. New Delhi: Atlantic, 2008, p. 170.
40. Jonathan Raban, "Losing the Owl, Saving the Forest," *New York Times*, June 26, 2010. www.nytimes.com.
41. Quoted in David Helvarg, *The War Against the Greens*. Boulder, CO: Johnson, 2004, p. 54.

Chapter Four: New Commitments on Climate Change

42. Quoted in Meteor Blades, "Blast from the Past—James Hansen, 1988," *Daily Kos* (blog), January 14, 2008. www.dailykos.com.
43. Quoted in D'Vera Cohn, "Thousands at Rally Hear 'the Cry of the Earth,'" *Washington Post*, April 23, 1990. www.washingtonpost.com.
44. Intergovernmental Panel on Climate Change, *Climate Change: The IPCC Response Strategies*. Covelo, CA: Island Press.
45. Spencer Weart, "Government: The View from Washington, DC," American Institute of Physics, 2008. www.aip.org.
46. Quoted in Robert F. Kennedy Jr., "Crimes Against Nature," 2017. www.robertfkennedyjr.com.
47. Quoted in John F. Harris and Ellen Nakasima, "Gore's Greenness Fades," *Washington Post*, February 28, 2000. www.washingtonpost.com.
48. Quoted in Andrew C. Revkin, "'An Inconvenient Truth': Al Gore's Fight Against Global Warming," *New York Times*, May 22, 2006. www.nytimes.com.
49. Quoted in Jennifer Keishin Armstrong et al., "The Slideshow That Saved the World," *Grist*, 2017. https://grist.org.
50. Quoted in Adam Nagourney, "Gore Wins Hollywood in a Landslide," *The Caucus* (blog), *New York Times*, February 25, 2007. https://thecaucus.blogs.nytimes.com.
51. Quoted in Robinson Meyer, "An Inconvenient Time for *An Inconvenient Sequel*," *Atlantic*, July 26, 2017. www.theatlantic.com.

52. Barack Obama, "President Obama's Climate Action Plan," Perma.cc, January 20, 2017. https://perma.cc.
53. Quoted in Brad Plumer, "Obama Says Fracking Can Be a 'Bridge' to a Clean-Energy Future. It's Not That Simple," *Washington Post*, January, 29, 2014. www.washingtonpost.com.
54. Plumer, "Obama Says Fracking Can Be a 'Bridge' to a Clean-Energy Future."

Chapter Five: New Leaders Continue the Battle

55. Quoted in Elizabeth Shogren, "5 Key Takeaways from the Latest Climate Change Report," National Geographic, November 2, 2014. https://news.nationalgeographic.com.
56. Quoted in Shogren, "5 Key Takeaways from the Latest Climate Change Report."
57. Daisy Kendrick, "Don't Ignore Young People—We're the Key to Fighting Climate Change," *Guardian* (Manchester), June 13, 2017. www.theguardian.com.
58. Quoted in Coral Davenport, "Climate Is Big Issue for Hispanics, and Personal," *New York Times*, February 9, 2015. https://mobile.nytimes.com.
59. Quoted in Cecily Hilleary, "Native Americans Most at Risk from Impact of Climate Change," Voice of America, April 19, 2017. www.voanews.com.
60. Quoted in Tara Houska, "Native American Youth to Obama: 'Rezpect' Our Water," Indian Country Today, August 11, 2016. https://indiancountrymedianetwork.com.
61. Quoted in Bess Levin, "Donald Trump Says He's 'an Environmentalist,' Promptly Announces Plans to Destroy the Environment," *Vanity Fair*, January 24, 2017. www.vanityfair.com.
62. Xiuhtezcatl Martinez, *We Rise*. El Segundo, CA: Rodale, 2017, p. 40.
63. Kelsey Cascadia Juliana, "Meet the 21 Youth Plaintiffs," Our Children's Trust, 2017. www.ourchildrenstrust.org.
64. "*Juliana v. U.S.* Climate Lawsuit," Our Children's Trust, 2017. www.ourchildrenstrust.org.
65. Julia Olson et al., "First Amended Complaint for Declaratory and Injunctive Relief," US District Court, September 10, 2015. https://static1.squarespace.com.
66. Martinez, *We Rise*, p. 47.
67. Al Gore, "*An Inconvenient Sequel: Truth to Power* (2017) Movie Script," Springfield! Springfield!, 2017. www.springfieldspringfield.co.uk.

FOR FURTHER RESEARCH

Books

Jules Archer, *To Save the Earth: The American Environmental Movement*. New York: Sky Pony, 2016.

Marcia Amidon Lusted, ed., *Extreme Weather Events*. Farmington Hills, MI: Greenhaven, 2017.

Xiuhtezcatl Martinez, *We Rise*. El Segundo, CA: Rodale, 2017.

Meghan Rock, *Rachel Carson: Marine Biologist and Winner of the National Book Award*. New York: Cavendish Square, 2017.

Rebecca Stefoff, *The Environmental Movement: Then and Now*. North Mankato, MN: Capstone, 2018.

Internet Sources

Barack Obama, "President Obama's Climate Action Plan," Perma.cc, January 20, 2017. https://perma.cc/SB7B-PEKG.

Samantha Sanchez, "How the West Is Won: Astroturf Lobbying and the 'Wise Use' Movement," *American Prospect*, March–April 1996. http://prospect.org/article/how-west-won-astroturf -lobbying-and-wise-use-movement.

Kate Wheeling and Max Ufberg, "'The Ocean Is Boiling': The Complete Oral History of the 1969 Santa Barbara Oil Spill," *Pacific Standard*, April 18, 2017. https://psmag.com/news/the -ocean-is-boiling-the-complete-oral-history-of-the-1969-santa -barbara-oil-spill.

Websites

Climate Reality Project (www.climaterealityproject.org). This organization was founded by Al Gore to find climate-change solutions that can be realistically implemented in communities throughout the world. The website offers information about climate change and provides links for young people interested in joining the Climate Reality Leadership Corps.

Earth Guardians (www.earthguardians.org). Earth Guardians is a student organization made up of activists, artists, and musicians dedicated to empowering young people to take over as leaders of the environmental movement. The group's website features inclusive information about environmental issues and ongoing campaigns.

Natural Resources Defense Council (www.nrdc.org). The council is one of the leading environmental organizations in the world, with more than 3 million members. The group's website provides wide-ranging environmental information about climate change, communities, energy, food, oceans, and the wild.

Nelson Institute for Environmental Studies (www.nelsonearth day.net). This website, originally created by Earth Day founder and Wisconsin senator Gaylord Nelson, contains personal and official papers and historical essays about the making of the modern environmental movement.

Our Children's Trust (www.ourchildrenstrust.org). In 2015 this organization initiated a lawsuit against the US government on behalf of the youngest generation. The trust's website features information about the lawsuit and others in courts throughout the world.

US Global Change Research Program (www.globalchange .gov). This government-funded program, mandated by Congress in 1990, exists to help people understand and respond to human-induced climate change. The site contains extensive data on climate change for various regions of the United States compiled by thirteen federal agencies.